NARRATIVE PEDAGOGY

Studies in the
Postmodern Theory of Education

Shirley R. Steinberg
General Editor

Vol. 386

The Counterpoints series is part of the Peter Lang Education list.
Every volume is peer reviewed and meets
the highest quality standards for content and production.

PETER LANG
New York • Washington, D.C./Baltimore • Bern
Frankfurt • Berlin • Brussels • Vienna • Oxford

Ivor F. Goodson & Scherto R. Gill

NARRATIVE PEDAGOGY

Life History and Learning

PETER LANG
New York • Washington, D.C./Baltimore • Bern
Frankfurt • Berlin • Brussels • Vienna • Oxford

Library of Congress Cataloging-in-Publication Data

Goodson, Ivor.
Narrative pedagogy: life history and learning / Ivor F. Goodson, Scherto R. Gill.
p. cm. — (Counterpoints, studies in the postmodern theory of education; v. 386)
Includes bibliographical references and index.
1. Education—Biographical methods. 2. Discourse analysis, Narrative—Research.
3. Postmodernism and education. I. Gill, Scherto. II. Title.
LB1029.B55G66   371.39—dc22   2010046963
ISBN 978-1-4331-0892-1 (hardcover)
ISBN 978-1-4331-0891-4 (paperback)

Bibliographic information published by **Die Deutsche Nationalbibliothek**.
Die Deutsche Nationalbibliothek lists this publication in the "Deutsche
Nationalbibliografie"; detailed bibliographic data is available
on the Internet at http://dnb.d-nb.de/.

Cover design by David Wilson

© 2011 Peter Lang Publishing, Inc., New York
29 Broadway, 18th floor, New York, NY 10006
www.peterlang.com

Printed in the United States of America

To Simon

Contents

Acknowledgments

We should like to thank our colleague Heather Stoner for her whole-hearted involvement and support in this research, and our friend Prof. Garrett Thomson for a series of stimulating conversations, particularly on philosophical and moral issues.

We should also like to thank the Learning Lives project team for their insights and expertise as well as textual commentaries, especially Dr. Norma Adair for her work with regard to conceptual clarification and data collection and Liz Briggs for her unstinting and generous support in her work for the project.

In particular, we would like to thank the wide range of storytellers and research participants who have worked with us. Their co-operation and collaboration have combined friendship and fraternity; generosity and good will.

Most importantly, we want to thank the Guerrand-Hermès Foundation for Peace for believing in the importance of dialogue and conversation in research understanding and learning and for generously sponsoring the research and writing of this book.

Preface

Narrative learning from within and through relationships and encounters

This book grew from of a series of conversations between two scholars working on parallel projects and a later joint project involving life narratives. These conversations began in earnest in 2008. At this time, Ivor Goodson was working on the Learning Lives project funded by the Economic and Social Research Council (ESRC). This was a four-year longitudinal study of people's lives and life history narrations with a particular focus on learning episodes. In particular, Ivor was concerned to define and delineate what he calls 'narrative learning'. Meanwhile, Scherto Gill was developing a Masters programme where life narratives are integrated in teachers' education. Scherto was interested in how personal narratives can be an important site for meaning-making and learning.

Our conversations, while starting from narrative learning, moved quickly to explore reciprocal interests in narrative work as a dialogic encounter. Thus in this book, we particularly underline narrative as pedagogy from the point of view that it invokes a 'third voice', which is the voice of the collaboration between the people involved in the narrative encounter. We realised in these conversations, the book itself emerged as a 'third voice' in namely the joint voice arising from the collaborative encounter between Ivor and Scherto.

As the interlocutors of the conversations and as authors of this book, we share the same concern: for a long time learning has been perceived and presented as taking place beyond the personal domain of selfhood and subjectivity. In recent years many educators, including ourselves, have attempted to journey into the uncharted territory of the 'self' in teaching and learning. In this context, life narratives have been perceived as one of the major ways that a person can make sense and interpret meaning, thus enabling learning from within. This has been an exciting field for us to explore despite the risks and challenges.

Overall, our conversations and reflections summarised in this book attempt to explore four major concerns.

First, we want to re-focus the debate about the relationships between narrative, learning and personhood in the light of postmodernist interpretations. For us, the real challenge of a more 'decentred', 'fragmented', 'multiple', and ever 'shifting' sense of self lies in the individual's ability to make sense of past and present lived experiences in ways that support more coherent actions in the future. It particularly requires more rigour to negotiate meaning internally and with others.

Second, we want to draw attention to the citation that social research using narratives and life histories as substantive data in itself challenging social researchers' understanding of the notion of validity. What often seems a struggle and sometimes a burden for social researchers, for example trying to maintain distance and objectivity, is in effect both unrealistic and impossible. This is because the nature of narrative and life history research invites closeness between the researcher and his/her participants, researcher's personal involvement and interest in what is biographically meaningful for him/her, emotional and reciprocal engagement, and the researcher's reflexivity. It is true that perceiving social research in this way inevitably questions the form and nature of the knowledge generated. However, instead of avoiding what is obviously a minefield of research ethics, it is necessary to be open and to embrace the challenges and ambiguities. We would argue that the very open nature of narrative work is one of the virtues of such research, for in some other research forms, the ethical and social issues are obscured or buried in numerical and statistical 'mazes'.

Third, we think it is time to acknowledge that social research using in-depth narrative and life history interviews can be significant forms of intervention. When carried out with full awareness and respect through the collaboration between the researcher and her participants, it brings about important shifts in their understanding of self and motivations, and even a reflection on their places in the world can occur. We argue that this shift in understanding is part of learning in and from life, is ultimately about growth and becoming oneself in relation to others and the world around us.

Fourth, this gives us an opportunity to explore more explicitly the pedagogic process leading to meaningful changes and development in individuals. In arguing for a new form of what Goodson calls narrative learning (Goodson, Biesta, Tedder, & Adnair, 2010) we want to point out that as one of the major sites of self-construction, life narrative (research) is a site for learning. By focusing on learning in relation to personal narrative, Goodson and his colleagues maintain that some of the normal issues of learner engagement are sidestepped. Since the person is already engaged in narrative construction there is no issue of the relevance of the learning to be undertaken through externally-presented curricula. In this book, we want to further explore this kind of learning, especially how narrative as a pedagogic process can nurture, more explicitly, a positive shift in one's sense of self.

Whilst we are aware of the range of problems and pitfalls any pedagogic engagement encounters, this book starts with certain underpinning convictions. We believe that through focusing on life stories, learning often takes place within the inner narrative landscape of the learner. Acknowledging that life experience and life narration are an important source and reason for learning is a particular valedictory route for each person and their integrity. In turn, it offers an opportunity for a person to take responsibility for their own learning and development. Narrative pedagogy involves reflective self-construction and an ongoing pattern of periodic reflexivity. At its heart is the belief in an emergent and evolving 'moral self' which can mediate between selfhood and personal and social action.

While accepting that learning takes place from within, at the same time we are convinced that it is crucial for learning to be embedded in the relationships and deeper encounters where it also takes place. Pedagogic intention is important, and creating a trusting and safe space is the key to an open atmosphere where individuals feel comfortable to share their lived experiences in narratives. This is where we encounter each other as human beings on many levels: cognitive, discursive, emotional and spiritual.

We want to stress the social and collective respects of narrative process in ways that honour both the internal and external process of human understanding and learning.

Organisation of the book

This book is divided into two parts: Part I reviews the existing use of narrative as research methodology and this part consists of four chapters.

Chapter One is an overview of the key concepts in life history and narrative work, highlighting the central notion of narrative identity.

Chapter Two reviews the narrative turn and its impact on the concepts underpinning narrative and life history research. It also introduces different approaches to narrative and life histories as research inquiry and points out challenges confronting researchers, especially those concerning research ethics. Discussed here are some uses of narrative as methodological approaches and as research data in different disciplines.

The first two chapters lay the conceptual framework for narrative as research methodology, including establishing the crucial point about the relationship between narrative and personal identity.

Chapter Three offers an opportunity to closely examine the narrative and life history research process using our existing research experience as examples and contexts. It describes the interview conversations, collaborative analysis and interpretation and the process of moving from life narratives to life history. It also poses and explores key questions in the field, such as who is interpreting whose stories and what really happens to the inner worlds of individuals when their narratives are extrapolated, analysed, interpreted and re-created in the research.

Chapter Four further reflects on the change, even transformation, or lack of it in an individual's understanding as the result of the narrative and life history research intervention. We draw once again on our research experience and put forward a proposition that different lifestory tellers have different narrative capacities and characteristics. These can determine how far a person is reflective and analytical when telling and re-constructing their life narratives.

In Part II, we explore the learning or changes that take place as the outcomes of the narrative encounter and establish narratives as pedagogic sites for learning.

Chapter Five investigates the nature of narrative encounters in the light of Gadamer's philosophical hermeneutics and Ricoeur and others' discussion on the ethics of narrative identity. We stress the importance of whole-person encounters, especially the part emotions play in learning as well as relationships and reciprocity in learning. In particular, we begin to look at questions such as: 'How does narrative encounter change an individual's understanding of their lived experience and meanings?' and, 'In what way does narrative link to a person's sense of identity and his/her actions in the world?'

Chapter Six pursues answers to these questions by looking at the movement and shifts in the narratives that individuals have constructed. It analyses the individual and social nature of life narratives, and how social forces and power dynamics shape and reshape the process of narrative construction. Our analysis confirms some of the arguments (reviewed in the first two chapters) that narrative encounter has the potential to transform a person's understanding of him/herself, their narratives, and above all, to change a person's courses of action and align them to the individual's values and purpose in life.

Chapter Seven moves from the concept of narrative learning to constructing a theory of narrative pedagogy. It critiques the narrowness of existing concepts of learning, distinguishes narrative learning from similar notions such as transformative learning, and points out that narration and narrative learning work in tandem. Hence, narrative as pedagogy is more than a technique for teaching or transmission; instead narrative pedagogy embraces the educator/facilitator's identity and integrity, and involves among other things, reciprocal narrative sharing, a caring relationship, respect and love. *Xr Indigenous pedagogy*

Chapter Eight brings us back to where we started, and revisits some of the salient conceptual, methodological and pedagogical points made in this book. In doing so, we focus on the important role narrative plays in one's selfhood, particularly in developing a moral self. It offers narrative pedagogy in teaching and learning within a community by an example of peer-to-peer narrative learning in teacher education. It also investigates the use of narrative in other group and collective contexts and how, by transforming memories and understanding, narrative helps to change the way that groups or communities interact and co-exist within a society. Narrative reconstruction is therefore not only an individual process of creating a new set of stories of the self and new moral self, but also a process that can provide a basis for groups and communities to consolidate their sense of integrity and wellbeing.

A note on the structure of the chapters

We regard this book as a learning endeavour since it arose from a series of conversations we have had over the space of two years. It gives us an opportunity to reflect on our respective research and teaching experiences as well as our collaborative project. Therefore organisation of the book and the structure of the chapters attempts to show this process of our own dialogic understanding.

In each chapter where necessary and possible, we insert an example of personal narrative that we involve in co-developing either through research or teaching. We try to offer examples of narratives from different voices-direct excerpts from an individual's narrative, co-composed texts and summaries written from a researcher's point of view.

Towards the end of each chapter, where possible, we have included a short exchange between ourselves the authors. The dialogue aims to share with the reader our own learning and to show that the writing in itself is not closed but an ongoing open process.

Each chapter ends with further questions for discussion and suggested reading. We hope this makes the text more digestible, playful, and more interactive.

Our hope is that the structure of this book mirrors the learning spiral of narration — the ongoing spiral of narrative processes. By a spiral process, we mean constant revisits and re-engagement with previous learning and ongoing meaning-making, which engenders new insights in a continuous progression towards better understanding.

Part I: Narrative as Research Methodology

1

The Concept of Narrative

Then we must first of all, it seems, supervise the storytellers. We'll select their stories whenever they are fine and beautiful and reject them when they aren't. And we'll persuade nurses and mothers to tell their children the ones we have selected, since they will shape their children's souls with stories much more than they will shape their bodies by handling them.

—Plato, Republic, Book 2, 377c

Introduction

This chapter presents an overview of the current literature on the use of life narratives in social research and the study of human life. We will examine some of the literature within a number of disciplines including sociology, education, and the literary field, for instance, life-story writing and biographical work. The review is intended to place narrative work within both a conceptual and a methodological context.

In the space below, we first introduce the main concepts that have been used in the existing literature and discuss the possible assumptions behind the different ways in which these concepts are defined and employed. This allows us to look at the philosophical underpinning of using life narratives in social research and in the studies of human life.

1. Life and narratives

Narratives and stories are sometimes used interchangeably in social research. Here is one definition:

> Narratives (stories) in the human sciences should be defined provisionally as discourses with a clear sequential order that connect events in a meaningful way for a definite audience and thus offer insights about the world and/or people's experiences of it (Hinchman & Hinchman, 1997, p. xvi)

In this definition, three common features shared by narratives and stories are highlighted:

1. temporality—all narratives encompass a sequence of events;

2. meaning—personal significance and meaning are externalised through the telling of lived experiences;

3. social encounter—all narratives are told to an audience and will inevitably be shaped by the relationship between the teller and the listener.

Another way of characterising narrative, from a discursive perspective was proposed by Gergen (1998). The author proposes that it contains the following features:

1. a value point, or an outcome of significance. This is connected to meaning or meaningfulness, but Gergen argues that the point of a story is that it must have value, which are determined by the teller of the tale and are connected to the cultural traditions within which the story takes place.

2. the events selected are relevant to the endpoint. Gergen perceives narratives as demanding 'ontological consequences' — the tellers of tales are not free to include all events, but only those that contribute to the conclusion.

3. the ordering of events. This is linked to temporality as described above, but Gergen further explains, using Bakhtin's (1981) words, that temporal order is determined by the need for the 'representability of events', which is connected to points (1) and (2).

4. stability of identities. This feature suggests that characters in stories tend to be present with a somewhat continuous or coherent identity over time, unless the story explains any changes.

5. causal linkages. The selection of events is aimed at presenting an explanation so that all plots and the endpoint are causally linked.

6. demarcation signs. Gergen sees this feature as different from the temporal characterisation above and referring to the beginning and ending of a story.

Clearly, Hinchman & Hinchman's definition and characterisation of narratives stress the significance of social interaction in the construction of narratives, and the transformation of human experience into meaning. (In Chapter Five we discuss the nature of narrative encounters in more detail.) In contrast, Gergen focuses his attention on the structure of a story and the organisation of plots and how they are constructed through the inherent value or meaning the storyteller assumes. We suspect that these two conceptions of narrative — one with an emphasis on social encounter and the other on story structure — help to explain the crucial and major differences between the life history approach to understanding narratives, and the narrative approach to inquiring into stories. (We examine the differences more closely in Chapter Two.)

However, these characterisations of life narratives illustrated here, although different, share a common assumption that there is an important connection between life as lived and life as told in personal narratives. Indeed, the connection between human life and narrative has been discussed from a number of philosophical perspectives, in particular, from a hermeneutic point of view. Some thinkers have argued that life and narratives are internally related and that human life is interpreted in narratives (see MacIntyre, 1981; Ricoeur, 1988, 1992). According to these authors, human life can be perceived as a process of narrative interpretation. In other words, life is meaningful, but the meaning is implicit and can become explicit in narrative and through narration. The hermeneutic interpretation of narratives is rooted in different schools of thought, including Gadamer's dialogic approach to hermeneutic understanding resulting in a 'fusion of horizons'. We return to this in later discussions especially in Chapter Five.

Let us now return to the definition of life narrative and why it is an important concept to explore. Broadly, there are three main reasons why sociologists are drawn to comparing life as lived and life as narrative.

Firstly, narrative has been perceived to be an inherently human concept. According to Roland Barthes, narrative is present in every age, in every place, in every society; it begins with the very history of mankind and there nowhere is nor has been a people without narrative (Barthes, 1975 p. 79).

Similarly, Ricoeur (1984), life, and in some senses even time, becomes human in and through narrative. Human life has always been deeply embedded in a web of narratives which in turn allow individuals, communities, cultures and nations to express who they are, where they have been, how they have lived and what they aspire to. Narrative is considered central to being human because much of our sense of purpose and meaning, selfhood, values and aspirations are based on our narratives (Grassie, 2008), and narratives are essential for humans to construct coherence and continuity in life (Taylor, 1989). At the same time, narrative also allows the possibility for individuals to adapt, modify and shift their stories and thereby lived experiences can be transformed.

Secondly, human life, whilst sometimes orderly, is often chaotic; whereas narratives, through their plots and temporality, allow individuals to assume a certain structure and configuration in their lives. This has made it possible for humans to develop direction and unity of action (MacIntyre, 1984). MacIntyre believes that narratives can help to explain human actions. He argues that in the telling of their lives, individuals place actions in the context of intentions 'with reference to their role in the history of the setting or settings in which they belong' (*ibid.*, p. 208). This is a reflexive process where individuals take the opportunity to 'write a further part' of their histories. In this way, in the narrative construct, human actions are united with their intention, values and purposes. When life is narrated, it is also lived, according to its narrative construction. Life becomes 'enacted narratives' (*ibid.*). This consolidates a mutually constitutive relationship between life and narrative: life forms the fundamental basis of narrative, and narrative provides order, structure and direction in life, and helps develop meanings in richer and more integrated ways.

Thirdly, sociologists are interested in pursuing the complex relationship between life and narrative because this relationship has profound implications for another concept, which happens to be primarily yet another narrative construct—self-identity. Identity itself can never be seen simply as a psychological concept. Rather, it is simultaneously cultural, historical, social and personal.

Identity, as a concept, has been defined from multiple perspectives. At times diverse definitions, and sometimes lack of definition, have caused certain confusions. Nevertheless, identity and narrative are intrinsically connected, and it is necessary that we review briefly some of these definitions before offering our own understanding of this concept.

2. The concept of identity from narrative perspectives

Identity is a concept often theorised differently in the various disciplines of psychology, anthropology, cultural studies, sociology and psycho-therapy. Our definition of the concept positions our view of identity primarily within life narratives, in other words, in narrative identity, which allows it to be situated at the junction of several disciplines.

Narrative identity is a notion put forward by Paul Ricoeur and hence has been used widely in studies of human lives. Narrative identity is a statement about an individual or a group of people in terms of "'who did what?'; "Who is the agent, the author?'" (Ricoeur, 1988, p. 246). Ricoeur asserts that 'self understanding is an interpretation, the self, in turn, finds in the narrative' (1992, p. 114). He explores the relationship between time and narrative and concludes that there is no thought about time except for the narrative of time, which links phenomenological time and cosmological time (1988, p.241–244).

Ricoeur suggests that the self contains two notions of identity at the same time: idem-identity and ipse-identity. Whilst not the most felicitous of phrases, idem-identity, the persisting self, Ricoeur describes as 'keeping one's promise', which includes genetic identification and the self in terms of physical and metaphysical continuity; whereas ipse-identity is selfhood, the very answer to the question of 'who I am', and is not dependent on anything permanent for its existence. Thus an individual's character is:

> the set of distinctive marks which permit the re-identification of a human being as the same. By the descriptive features that will be given, the individual compounds numerical identity and qualitative identity, uninterrupted continuity and permanence in time (Ricoeur 1992, p. xx).

The self characterised by 'ipse-identity' or 'self-sameness' is continuously adjusted by narrative configurations in the telling of one's life stories, and reading and listening to one's narrative. Ricoeur maintains that narratives play an important mediating role between a number of dialectics, including harmony and dissonance in human experience, narrative as lived and narrative as told; narrative as innovation and sedimentation, as fact and fiction; what is and what ought to be; the exalted cogito and shattered cogito; the person as the interpreter and the interpreted, as the reader and the writer of one's own life; and finally, the lived world and the told world.

Ricoeur argues that to answer the question, 'Who?' is to tell the story of a life, and thus, narrative identity, 'constitutive of self-consistency, can include change, mutuality, within the cohesion of one life time' (Ricoeur, 1988, p. 246). Similarly, McAdams (1996, p. 307) sees it as 'an internalized and evolving narrative of the self that incorporates the reconstructed past, perceived present and anticipated future'. It thus allows the individual to live a life in a continuum.

Narrative identity defined and elaborated in this way does not reject consistency and coherence in self-identity, nor does it exclude the possibility of shifts, changes and transformation. By contrast, consistency and coherence in identity are the main challenge that poststructuralists and postmodernists put forward in the light of personal identity. According to Sarup (1993), postmodernity means after modernity. It refers to the incipient or actual dissolution of those social forms associated with modernity. Postmodern thinking tends to perceive the self as decentred and multiple, implying an anxiety about identity (Turkle, 1995). By this view, identity is constantly shifting according to the changes in time, audience, and perception.

Where does narrative identity stand in postmodernist thinking?

Let us briefly examine the progression from modernity to postmodernity as a starting point to see how identity is perceived the post-modern era. Lyotard (1979) pointed out that postmodernity occurred when the enlightenment project of 'grand narratives', of progression, emancipation, and growth had been abandoned. Instead of grand narratives, Lyotard called for a series of mini-narratives (les petites recits) that are 'provisional, contingent, temporary, and relative', providing an argument for the breakdown of overarching beliefs and values. This fragmentation therefore also applies in self-identity. The self is no longer perceived as fixed, unitary and essentialised. Instead, self is always subject to deconstruction.

Rob Stones (1996, p. 22) captures the characteristics of the postmodern approach to social sciences thus:

1. Respect for the existence of a plurality of perspectives, as against a notion that there is one single truth from a privileged perspective;

2. Local, contextual studies in place of grand narratives;

3. Emphasis on disorder, flux and openness, as opposed to order, continuity and restraint.

Other authors have examined possible reasons why grand narratives, and authorities, are being abandoned. For instance, according to Lyon (2000), postmodernity is characterised by two elements: the rise of new media technologies, and the dominance of consumerism in society.

According to Lyon, new media technologies make it possible for traditional authorities to be questioned and challenged by the individual, and the non-authoritarian messages broadcast through modern media blur the boundaries between 'reality' and projected 'images'. The result is a profusion of different frames for individuals to use for the construction of their experience and to thus shape their identities. Under such conditions, the notion of identity becomes fragmentary and unstable.

At the same time, the strong influence of consumerism in society, 'the power of consumption' provides further opportunities for individuals to re-define themselves, and for a person to have a 'plastic self'. In this way identity becomes as flexible as possible, in order to experience as much as possible and to create the 'expressive self' that seeks authenticity and the completion of the inner-narrative.

Thus the self is multi-faceted, according to the individual's construction of how the self is to be perceived in particular contexts, that is, a predetermined role within which persons can shape their experience. This works with consumer choices and media influence. The combination of these two influences results in identity coming to the foreground as a question that has no final answer. This is both a source of exhilaration, i.e., individuals seem to be free to construct themselves, and a source of anxiety because people are no longer clear about who they are at the deepest level.

Post-structuralists further posit the self within the construct of language and discourse. Thus identity is regarded as being conditioned by language; and since discourse itself is fluid, and hence language, this further de-stabilises the individual's sense of self. Identity becomes a way of talking about the self, a fluctuating and fluid discursive force (Butler, 1990; Foucault, 1972). In this sense, identity is communicated in our interactions with each other, which is shifting, and temporary, depending on the context within which the discourse takes place. Identity is also constructed through a process of interaction between people and institutions, and the concepts of time and space/location must be taken into account when discussing identity.

Postmodernists particularly stress the notion that identity is a construction through the dynamic circulation of power resulting in shifting discursive fields. The complex relationships between power and discourse allow feminists to explore identity and 'gendered meanings' in a new light. For the first time, identity (as in gender identity) is seen as an enactment, a performance, and, in Judith Butler's words, identity is a narrative that is upheld by 'the tacit collective agreement to perform, produce, and sustain discrete and polar genders as cultural fictions which is obscured by the credibility of those productions—and the punishments that attend not agreeing to believe in them', (Butler, 1999, p. 140).

Erving Goffman[1] also perceives the self as performed character. He says:

> It is not an organic thing that has a specific location, whose fundamental fate is
> to be born, to mature, and to die; it is a dramatic effect arising diffusely from a
> scene that is presented (Goffman, 1959, pp. 252/3).

Although this notion of performed identity is different from the construct of
relational self put forward by other feminist writers such as Carol Gilligan (1982),
Nancy Chodorow (1986) and Dana Jack (1991), the fundamental premises of the
claim is the same—the challenge to the modernist conception of an essential core
self that is autonomous.

Critiques of postmodernist thinking point out that a postmodernist approach
to understanding identity and subjectivity, lays sometimes disproportionate emphasis on the instability of subjectivity, presenting the subject as a fiction, a fantasy;
or as invention/product through fixing identity using power and 'policing'
(Hekman, 2000). Hekman sees this situation as stalemate because:

> On one hand, the feminist theorists influenced by poststructuralism and postmod-
> ernism advocate a fluid, constructed identity, eschewing the fixing of identity as
> a modernist fiction that is both false and dangerous. On the other hand, the prac-
> titioners of identity politics, in the process of constructing a new, more palatable
> identity, inadvertently fix that identity; they police their members internally by
> enforcing a certain identity and police them externally by presenting a united,
> falsely homogeneous front in the political world that allows a policing of subjects
> by the state. Ambiguous, fluid identities don't fly in the political world or in courts
> of law. Thus, far from problematizing the connection between identity and pol-
> itics as the theorists had hoped, identity politics has instead made embracing a spe-
> cific, fixed identity a precondition for political action (*ibid.*, p. 297).

Hekman also notes that the multiplicity of identity does not allow the harmonious co-existence of all the identities in one person. It makes it impossible for the
individual to bring all the 'selves' to the table at the same time.

The concerns expressed about some postmodernist conception of the self
seem to focus on two major themes. Both of these are of considerable importance
with regard to narrative identity. The first set of concerns focuses on the very sources
of the self—a subject that Charles Taylor has written about with great elegance. The
second is connected to the issue of human aspiration and action amidst a world of
chaos, fragmentation and plurality.

It is true that whilst traditional boundaries are breaking down, individuals no longer simply draw their identity from sources such as clan, institution, culture, ethnicity, nation and other roots. Nowadays, people belong to diverse groups, and one person may simultaneously belong to a number of collectives. Race, gender, ideology, parents, family, education, workplace, media, politics, religion and nationality simultaneously impact on the way individuals construct their identity. Sarup states:

> Human subjects have the capacity to 'work' on these differences within an individual, who is never a unified member of a single unified group. It is these very differences that create the space in which the human subject exercises a measure of interpretative freedom (1996 p. 25).

Identity is constantly reconstituted in accordance with the collectives one identifies oneself with at particular moments in time (cf. Wenger, 1998 on communities of practice). Some scholars have pointed out that postmodernist thinkers do not necessarily distinguish identity from social membership and role. Castells (1997, pp. 6/7) further explains that 'for a given individual, or for a collective actor, there may be a plurality of identities'. However, he also cautions us of the possible impact of mixing roles and identities, by maintaining that 'such a plurality is a source of stress and contradiction in both self representation and social action' (*ibid.*). This is because identity must be distinguished from what, traditionally, sociologists have called roles and role sets. Roles are defined by norms structured by the institutions and organisations of society. The relative weight of risks in influencing people's behaviour depends upon the negotiations and arrangements between individuals and those institutions and organisations (*ibid.*).

Hekman (2000) draws on Glass (1993) and argues that, 'the postmodern conception of self and identity is dangerous in the sense that it describes the fragmented, shattered selves of multiple personality disorders' (Heckman, 2000 p. 298).

This leads to the second concern. No doubt the concept of identity from the social and discursive point of view contrasts with that of psychological concepts which often emphasise the distinct personality of the individual as an enduring or persisting entity, the definition of which focuses on the inner coherence and unity of the person as a whole. However, as pointed out by Castells, a hybridised and multiplicity of identity does not account for human acts and coherent agency. Indeed, without a stable sense of self, it would be impossible for individuals to consolidate their choices and actions.

The question that interests us is: will the rejection of the unitary and coherent identity allow life history research participants to use narration as a tool in the search for coherence? We believe that most people narrate their lives in an attempt to achieve coherence. This way of socially constructing the self is crucial for identifying individual and collective actions. We want to highlight here that life history work focuses on the actual way individuals narrate their lives, rather than the way they should. Therefore life history work seeks to avoid the fate of some postmodern fundamentalists.

One of the central paradoxes of postmodernity is that the more fluidity, flexibility and multiplicity is on offer, the more the individual might seek a sense of security and coherence as a bulwark and personal anchor. Thus Hekman argues for a 'middle ground on the constitution of the subject, a doer who is neither essential nor the embodiment of a universal substance, but nevertheless possesses a stable concept of self' (*ibid.*, p. 298).

Giddens (1991) offers a different thesis in terms of the complex changes experienced in the 21st century. He observes the new era as high modernity in contrast to post modernity. According to Giddens, postmodernity (although he uses the term 'high modernity') refers to societies where modernity is well developed, and which are post-traditional, but where many features of modernity still hold. Key aspects of such modern social life are characterised by 'profound processes of the reorganisation of time and space, . . . and social relations free from the hold of specific locales, . . . across wide time-space distances' (*ibid.*, p. 2). In his writing Giddens (1990, 1991) further identifies radical doubt, uncertainty, multiple choices, and the re-examination and re-application of trust and risk as features of postmodernity. These features result in changes to moral priorities, the interconnections between an individual's private (personal) and public (social) life; the relationships between knowledge and social institutions, and between human agents and their choices; and above all, modes and opportunities for the understanding and construction of self-identity.

Thus Giddens maintains that within these complex operations, the self in high modernity becomes a reflexive project:

> In the post-traditional order of modernity, and against the backdrop of new forms of mediated experience, self-identity becomes a reflexively organised endeavour. The reflexive project of the self, which consists in the sustaining of coherent, yet continuously revised, biographical narratives, takes place in the multiple choices . . . (1991, p. 5)

Giddens further holds that persons' self-identity is fundamental to their ontological security, which is at the same time both 'robust' and 'fragile'. It is robust because it 'is often securely enough held where major tensions or transitions in the social environments within which the person moves'; and it is fragile because 'the biography the individual reflexively holds in mind is only one "story" among many other potential stories that could be told about her development as a self' (*ibid.*, pp. 54–55). Giddens stresses the significance of maintaining the continuity of self-identity in the everyday world and sees a person's self-identity as found in her capacity to '*keep a particular narrative going*' (*ibid*, p. 54).

On this point Giddens agrees with Charles Taylor and writes that, 'In order to have a sense of who we are, we have to have a notion of how we have become, and of where we are going' (*ibid.*). In this sense what Giddens calls a, 'reflexive project' is not merely a narcissistic obsession of the ego, but also involves an understanding of what it means to be a 'person', which applies to both the self and others, and the concept of the person facilitates the individual's capacity to 'use 'I' in shifting contexts' (*ibid.*, p. 53).

Personal meaning is paradoxically being placed at the centre of the search in postmodernity. What Giddens terms 'existential isolation' continues to raise moral issues and calls for 'life politics' which are 'concerned with human self-actualisation, both on the level of individual and collectively' (*ibid*, p. 9).

At this juncture, let us to return to our earlier discussion of the concern about human action. This is where narrative identity can provide an entry point for a discussion on the 'value-generating capacities' of narrative functions (Gergen, 1998). To take a closer look, several authors support the connection between life narratives and the development of the moral or ethical self. Ricoeur, in the conclusion of 'Time and Narrative', suggests that

> the self of self-knowledge is not the egotistical and narcissistic ego whose hypocrisy and naivety the hermeneutics of suspicion have denounced, along with its aspects of an ideological superstructure and infantile and neurotic archaism. The self of self-knowledge is the fruit of an examined life . . . (Ricoeur, 1988, p. 247).

The ethical self or moral identity is further placed by Ricoeur within its culture and community. Similarly, Taylor also places human narratives and human storytelling within an ethical domain. He argues that identity is to be defined by 'the commitments and identifications' which provide the 'frame or horizon' within which the individual can try to 'determine from case to case what is good, or valuable, or what ought to be done', or what a person endorses or opposes. In other words, to define one's identity is to determine the horizon within which one is capable of 'taking a stand' (Taylor, 1989, p. 27).

Taylor's argument for the taking of a (moral) stand within a horizon is also sum-marised in MacIntyre's thesis that includes the community in an individual's moral identity:

> Man is in his actions and practice, as well as in his fictions, essentially a story-telling animal. He is not essentially, but becomes through his history, a teller of stories that aspire to truth. But the key question for men is not about their own authorship; I can only answer the question "What am I to do" if I can answer the prior question "Of what story or stories do I find myself a part?"(MacIntyre, 1984, p. 211)

Hence, our narrative identity clarifies that what is good for me has to be good for those communities that I am part of. Ricoeur further suggests that the notion of narrative identity can be applied to both individuals and communities because individuals and communities are 'constituted in their identity by taking up narra-tives that become for them their actual history' (1988, p. 247).

3. Challenges to the notion of narrative identity

Given the above articulation of the relationship between life, narrative and our extended discussion of narrative identity, there remain a number of issues and con-cerns with these concepts.[2]

The first set of problems concern self-perception. If a person is constructing identity through life stories, then he/she can do so as they please, denying the pos-sible risk of making an error or constructing an identity that is false. Such effort to understand oneself excludes the possibility of misunderstanding. This chal-lenge is not the same as the typical criticism of social constructivism in that the self and the world are perceived through their interaction with each other. This is a fun-damentally philosophical question which requires the kind of treatment that this book does not afford.

The second set of problems concern self-authorship. If as argued by Ricoeur and others, life is storied, and each person is his own author, it is this dichotomis-ing of the person and his life which is potentially problematic. The relationship between a person and his/her life is much more intimate than the relationship between an author and a story that he/she writes. Even though one could have lived differently (after his/her narration), one's life is still a person in time. It is not *some-thing distinct* from me in the way that a story is from its author.

The third set of problems concerns narratives or story's *raison d'être*. A story is basically an artefact created to be read, and similarly narratives are told to an audi-ence. Their construction is shaped by the concerns and interests of the potential readership. It would be a degrading mistake to think of oneself as an object that exists solely for the sake of an audience. It is equally absurd to think of oneself and one's life as a film or as a set of images and stories.

In addition to the above problems, there are misleading aspects in this conception. For instance, many stories have certain basic plots but real life is much more ambiguous. For example, a plot might be that the hero returns home in glory. But, in reality, no one is really purely a hero or a villain. Our real life characters are much more ambiguous and fragmented. Stories are often morally black and white, but even with shades of grey added in, our lives are not necessarily overwhelmingly moral. In other words, a moral sense is not the only, or even the main, dimension of assessment we use in our everyday lives. For most people, life is not morally driven in the way that stories usually are. By moral, we mean that stories are told to instil a particular value and promote certain ideas or behaviours.

Furthermore, an understanding of oneself is necessarily much more complex and richer than any story or character in a story. There is always more that could be said or than what has been said. This implies that the notion of a story or even a set of narratives is insufficient to capture our understanding of ourselves.

A person could think that he or she is living out a certain plot and act and anticipate accordingly, but real life is always uncertain. So the chaotic, ambiguous and uncertain nature of human life presents a big challenge to narrative researchers and life historians, whose task mainly focuses on making sense of the lived experience of individuals through collaborating with their participants in interpreting and analysing their narratives. However, it is precisely because of these challenges that narrative and life histories have become an exciting topic to explore.

Questions for discussion

Postmodernist thinking challenges the notion a sense of self that is coherence-seeking. A number of the authors reviewed in this chapter, when discussing the notion of narrative identity, have set up what we have called the paradox of postmodernity. In other words, at a time of chaos, fragmentation and plurality, far from embracing the notion of multiplicity, individuals are compelled to respond by searching for coherence and continuity.

The paradox of postmodernity further poses challenges to narrative and life history researchers. As we have pointed out, and shall continue to explore in the following chapters, meaning-making and having a coherent sense of oneself are crucial for an individual's integrity and for identifying a course of action in the world that shows congruence with one's identity.

As we shall argue later it is important to not only distinguish between the 'internal' affairs of selfhood in one's narratives and their 'external' relations in the world at large but also to build a bridge between internal affairs and external relations in order to exercise one's agency.

For now, the following questions might be helpful in consolidating some of the ideas we have put forward in this chapter:

- How does one understand the relationship between narrative and identity?
- What are the particular characteristics encompassed in the concept of 'narrative identity'?
- How have life narratives and identity politics changed in the transition from modernity to postmodernity?

Howard Becker (1977) says that each person develops a 'moral career' during their life course.

- What is the relationship between a person's 'moral career' and their life narrative?
- What are the main challenges to, and concerns with, the notion of narrative identity in light of one's moral career?

Further Reading

Atkinson, R. (1998). *The life story interview.* Thousand Oaks, CA: Sage.

Birren, J., & Cochran, K. (2001). *Telling the stories of life through guided autobiography groups.* Baltimore, MD: Johns Hopkins University Press.

Church, O. M., & Johnson, M. L. (1995). Worth remembering: The process and products of oral history. *International History of Nursing Journal, 1*(1), 19–31.

Gergen, K. J. (1996). Beyond life narratives in the therapeutic encounter. In J. E. Birren & G. M. Kenyon (Eds.), *Aging and biography: Explorations in adult development* (pp. 205–223). New York: Springer.

Polkinghorne, D. (1988). *Narrative knowing and the human sciences.* Albany, NY: SUNY Press.

Sennett, R. (1998). *The corrosion of character: The personal consequences of work in the new capitalism.* New York: W.W. Norton.

2

The Narrative Turn
in Social Research

Indeed this was originally the claim of social science—to be neutral, cut off, objective. Researchers took their 'subjects' as 'objects'—probing and prodding, poking and peeking, testing and measuring as if they were studying molecules or mice rather than ethically engaged human beings.

—Kenneth Plummer, *Documents of Life 2*, 2001, p. 205

Introduction

In this chapter, we revisit the 'narrative turn', briefly review its history and explore its growing popularity, and the reason behind it. We then examine two major approaches to narrative work: narrative inquiry and life history research. In so doing, we also identify some similarities and differences that researchers and writers in the field have pointed out about these two methods. Furthermore, we go through some of the challenges of narrative and life history as qualitative research methodologies and flag up some of the many ethical issues that confront researchers in the field. Lastly, we give a brief overview about the use of narrative and life history methodologies in different disciplines.

1. The 'narrative turn' in social research

Over the last few decades, social researchers have shown an increasing interest in individuals and groups' narratives or stories. This is what many social scientists refer to as the 'narrative turn' (Polkinghorne, 1988; Czarniawska, 2004; Herman, Jahn & Ryan, 2005). Some of these authors claim that narratives have their origins in narratology, hermeneutics, structuralism and literary tradition including discourse analysis and feminism. Indeed, the 'narrative turn' has emerged in the context of a new wave of philosophical discussion on the relationships between self, other, community, social, political and historical dynamics. It also includes questioning and challenging the positivist approach to examining the social world and understanding human experience.

Major criticism of the positivist approach focuses on the fact that it does not allow human actions and social interaction to be properly scrutinised or represented. Positivist research tends to place the 'observer' or 'researcher' of social phenomena outside the social reality, independent from the very social and historical fabric of which they are a part, and thereby posing problems in understanding that reality. But, such complex dynamics do not simply exist 'out there' in the objective world; rather they are the outcome of socially and historically mediated human consciousness. Furthermore, the positivist approach to examining and representing the social world does not necessarily interrogate the status quo and by this absence can offer tacit normative support.[1]

Critical theorists often argue that positivism lacks the reflexive element necessary to investigate the complex relationships within the social world. Some have 'called for a sociology that grappled with the intersection of biography and history in society and the ways in which personal troubles are related to public issues' (Berger & Quinney, 2004, p. 4). Therefore the narrative turn arose at a time of a pressing need for self-reflexive modes of inquiry into the social phenomena that encompass individuals' personal and collective biographies and social history (Giddens, 1991; Taylor, 1991). This transition is inseparable from our earlier exploration of developments in the theorisation of narrative identity, especially with regard to the emerging new approaches to studying the self in the social worlds in the period of postmodernity.

It is difficult to pinpoint exactly when narrative and life history methods became part of the common usage amongst sociologists and social researchers and scholars in general, but anthropologists appear to have employed the first life histories in developing studies of in developing studies of American Indian chiefs at the beginning of the 20th century. In the period that followed, the method was increasingly adopted by scholars in the humanities, particularly by sociologists. The method has been subject to the normal waves of fashion that sweep through the academy, and there have been periods of high popularity followed by periods of substantial underuse.

As Martin Bulmer's (1984) magisterial study of the Chicago School shows, a major landmark in the development of life history came with the publication of Thomas & Znaniecki's (1918–1920) colossal work, *The Polish Peasant in Europe and America*. Through the exploration of Polish peasants' experience of migrating to the United States, Thomas and Znaniecki employed life histories to provide the 'personal flesh' of the migrant experience. This pioneering work established life history as a *bona fide* research tool within the Chicago School of sociology, and this position was consolidated by the flourishing tradition of sociological works stimulated in Chicago in the subsequent years particularly by Robert Park (Park, Burgess, & McKenzie, 1925; Park, 1952).

In a range of studies of city life completed under Park, the life history method was strongly employed, including: *The Gang* (Thrasher, 1927), *The Gold Coast and the Slum* (Zorbaugh, 1929), *The Hobo* (Anderson, 1923), *The Ghetto* (Wirth, 1928), to just mention a few. Perhaps the model for a life history study can be found in Clifford Shaw's account of a mugger in his book *The Jack-Roller* (Shaw, 1930). Howard Becker's comments on Shaw's study underline one of the major strengths of the life history method:

> By providing this kind of voice from a culture and situation that are ordinarily not known to intellectuals generally and to sociologists in particular, *The Jack-Roller* enables us to improve our theories at the most profound level: by putting ourselves inside Stanley's skin, we can feel and become aware of the deep biases about such people that ordinarily permeate our thinking and shape the kind of problems we investigate. By truly entering into Stanley's life, we can begin to see what we take for granted (and ought not to) in designing our research–what kind of assumptions about delinquents, slums and Poles are embedded in the way we set the questions we study (Becker, 1970, p. 71).

After reaching a peak in the 1930s the life history approach fell from grace and was largely abandoned by social scientists for the next several decades. Dollard produced one of the most important works on the methodological bases of life history in his book *Criteria for the Life History* (Dollard, 1949). Because Dollard was writing some time after a decline in life history methods, Dollard's work didn't receive the attention it deserved.

In the 1970s there was the beginning of resurgence (Plummer, 1990) when a series of studies had some resonance with the Chicago School's work. In the years that followed feminist researchers were particularly vociferous in their support of the approach, and the marvellous study 'Interpreting Women's Lives' by the Personal Narratives Group in 1989 led to a substantial rehabilitation of the method. With increasing focus on subjectivity, we can see how life history has once again come centre stage in social scientific work.

From the social research point of view, narrative is both the method of inquiry and the phenomenon (i.e., individuals leading storied lives) under research (Clandinin & Connelly, 2000). Narrative is found in a number of disciplines, from anthropology to psychiatry; from history to theology; from media studies to organisational research, from discourse analysis to the study of teachers' lives and teaching; from politics to healthcare, and so forth. It is also found in different epistemological positions including phenomenology, hermeneutics, constructivism, feminism, critical theories, etc. In this way, narratives also provide the opportunity for 'a mixed genre' in social research (Geertz, 1983).

Inquiring into life narratives combines a 'modern' interest in learning, understanding and a concern for agency and human action with 'postmodern' concerns such as discourse and power, 'forc(ing) the social sciences to develop new theories and new methods and new ways of talking about the self and society' (Denzin, 2004, p. xiii).

Narratives provide opportunities to gain insights into the lived experience of individuals and thus can illuminate an understanding of the 'field' or culture as a whole. This has always been what qualitative social researchers are interested in rather than abstract and decontextualised information and numerical data for computational analysis (Polkinghorne, 1992). Dollard (1949, p. 4) illustrated this point, claiming that 'detailed studies of the lives of individuals will reveal new perspectives on the culture as a whole which are not accessible when one remains on the formal cross sectional plane of observation'.

Detailed studies of individuals' lives also allow stories to function as political responses, broadcasting 'voices' that are excluded from or neglected within dominant political structures and processes. These new voices from people in previously marginalised groups bring to light their own 'truths' (which are inevitably multi-vocal) about the social systems and institutions as they experience them. Hence narratives unfold the depth and complexity of human experience, power and other social dynamics, enabling researchers to extend their analyses to consider multiple levels of the phenomenon under research (Plummer, 2001).

2. Narratives in social research

The potential for using life narratives in studying human experience has then long been recognised by sociologists and scholars from diverse disciplines. Despite the common appreciation of narrative in social research, there is also a huge divide between different ways of conceptualising the narrative approach to research, how stories are analysed, and relatively little concern about the research process and insufficient attention to the diverse ethical concerns embedded in it.

In this space, we intend to develop an overview of the different conceptions of the use of narrative in research and how each conception leads to other related questions. For this purpose, we borrow Ojermark's (2007) helpful summary of the terminology used in narrative and life history literature. Box 1 contains some of the items on her list which are relevant to this discussion.

Polkinghorne (1992) summarises a broad use of narrative in research inquiry that 'refers to a subset of qualitative research designs in which stories are used to describe human action' (1992, p. 5). From this perspective narrative involves any prosaic discourse, as described by Miles & Huberman (1994), which refers to any research data in the form of discourse including interviews, transcripts, field notes, reflective journals, as well as any other body of text that has been used to analyse and provide access to research themes, and also final research reports which could be in the form of narratives (about the study).

Box 1: Summary of terminology in narrative and life history research (after Ojermark, 2007, p. 4)

> **Biographical research:** Research undertaken into individual lives employing auto-biographical documents, interviews or other sources and presenting accounts in various forms (e.g., in terms of editing, written, visual or oral presentation, and some degree of researcher narration and reflexivity).
> **Family history:** The systematic narrative and research of past events relating to a specific family or specific families.
> **Narrative:** A story with a plot and existence separate from the life of the teller. Narrative is linked with time as a fundamental aspect of social action. Narratives provide the organisation for our actions and experiences, since we experience life through conceptions of the past, present and future.
> **Oral history:** Personal recollections of events and their causes and effects. Also refers to the practice of interviewing individuals about their past experiences of events with the intention of constructing an historical account.
> **Case history:** History of an event or social process, not of any person in particular.

Life history: Account of a life based on interviews and conversations. The life history is based on the collection of written or transcribed oral accounts requested by a researcher. The life story is subsequently edited, interpreted and presented in one of a number of ways, often in conjunction with other sources. Life histories may be topical, focusing on only one segmented portion of a life, or complete, attempting to tell the full details of a life as it is recollected. The life history offers a triangulated account employing the life narrative as recounted, other testimonies and historical documents.

Life story: The account of a person's story of his or her life, or a segment of it, as told to another. It is usually quite a full account across the length of life but may refer to a period or aspect of the life experience. When related by interview to the researcher it is the result of an interactive relationship.

Narrative inquiry: Similar to 'biographical research', or 'life history research', this term is a loose frame of reference for a subset of qualitative research that uses personal narratives as the basis of research. 'Narrative' refers to a discourse form in which events and happenings are configured into a personal unity by means of a plot.

Testimonio: The first-person account of a real situation that involves repression and maginalization.

As pointed out in Chapter One, other authors tend to regard narrative from a much more general prespective where it is seen as equivalent to a story, rather than falling into one of the categories mentioned in the box above. Polkinghorne (1988, 1992) believes that equating narrative to story holds 'significant promise' for social researchers. In this view, narratives or stories 'combine a succession of incidents into a unified episode' (Polkinghorne, 1995, p. 7). In the meantime, various art forms can contribute to the plots of stories in addition to oral telling or research interviewing—a dance, a film, or written document, such as a personal diary or letters.

In this book, we will return to this point repeatedly with regard to the major difference between prosaic discourse and narrative. We believe that the difference lies in who the subjects trying to make sense of their lived experience are. Prosaic discourse seems to emphasise the role of the researcher in identifying themes and constructing categories for an understanding of the causal effects and outcomes of human actions. In this case, the researchers' observation, interpretation and analysis of the participants' stories and experiences serve as the meaning and insights derived from the research. Narrative seems to rely on the storied nature embedded in human experience and the inherent meaning that participants to extrapolate by selecting events and creating an overarching plot. In this situation, the researcher would pursue vigorously the structure in the discourse of the story and, from the way the teller or the participant employs the events and the temporality of the plot, the researcher further collaborates with her participants and delineates meaning and understanding of events as narrated.

The ways narrative inquiries and life history research studies are conceptualised and conducted bear certain similarities. According to Hitchcock & Hughes (1995, p. 186), the research approach using life narratives 'facilitates a deeper appreciation of an individual's experience of the past, living with the present, and a means of facing and challenging the future'. Becker (1970) suggested that the life history approach is 'superior' to other methods because:

> it enables the research to build up a mosaic-like picture of the individuals and the events and people surrounding them so that relations, influences and patterns can be observed . . . (t)he retrospective quality . . . enables one to explore social processes over time and adds historical depth to subsequent analysis (quoted in Hitchcock & Hughes, 1995, p. 186).

Evident in this is these authors' conviction that narrative research is an umbrella term and life history is merely a technique within this broader research methodology. In particular, the authors define life histories as 'stories or narratives recalling events in an individual's life', and see life history, together with other qualitative oriented research such as ethnography, as constituting a 'life-story' approach in sociology (*ibid.*, p. 187).

Narrative and life history research are related and not necessarily distinct approaches. Here we want to discuss them together in order to prepare the ground for our ongoing argument about the need for a more contextualised approach to research life narratives. We focus our discussion on a comparison between Connelly & Clandinin's concept of narrative inquiry and Goodson's (2006) and Goodson & Sikes' (2001) elaboration of life history research.

According to Connelly & Clandinin narrative inquiry is the study of human experience of the world. The authors argue that life narrative 'names the structured quality of experience to be studied, and it names the patterns of inquiry for its study' (1990, p. 2). Therefore narrative goes both ways: on the one hand, 'people by nature lead storied lives and tell stories of those lives'; on the other hand, researchers inquire into such narratives, 'describe such lives, collect and tell stories of them, and write narratives of experience' (*ibid.*).

By concentrating on stories of the participants and the stories of the research, Connelly & Clandinin argue, (t)he central task is evident when it is grasped that people are both living their stories in an ongoing experiential text and telling their stories in words as they reflect upon life and explain themselves to others. For the researcher, this is a portion of the complexity of narrative, because a life is also a matter of growth toward an imagined future and, therefore, involves retelling stories and attempts at reliving stories. A person is, at once, engaged in living, telling, retelling, and reliving stories (*ibid,* p. 4).

In this way, the narratives of the participants' lived experience of the social world and of the researcher get entangled in the research process and thus share the 'narrative construction and re-construction' (*ibid.* p. 5). In this entanglement, multi-vocal reports and stories of multiple selves can bring forward multiple levels of understanding of the social context/world.

Connelly & Clandinin consider this unravelling process similar to narrative therapy because '(t)his way of approaching the event is aimed at reconstructing a story of the event from the point of view of the person at the time the event occurred' (*ibid.* p. 11). Indeed, this does sound similar to what is intended in narrative therapy, i.e., to re-author the stories (Epston & White, 1990). We will return to the distinction between narrative as research, narrative as pedagogy and narrative as therapy later in this book. What Connelly & Clandinin have proposed, following from the above, is the possibility that research participants and perhaps the researcher herself (although the authors do not give a clear indication of this) derive meaning from the stories and the storying process, and can begin to 'create a new story of self, which changes the meaning of the event, its description, and its significance for the larger life story the person may be trying to live' (*ibid.*). It is also a dialogic process in which the researcher constructs and re-constructs her own identity.

Elbaz (1990) pointed out that there is a difference between story being used as a 'methodological device' and as the research 'methodology itself'. In this regard, life history and narrative inquiry share a common path, i.e., a collaborative process of inquiry. where both the participants and the researcher acknowledge they are part of the phenomenon being studied and that their perceptions, values and worldview make up the inter-subjective exchange, and that wider social and cultural contexts are embedded in this. We believe that the act of narrative construction must be scrutinised against the historical and social contexts in a systematic manner. This is the major emphasis of life history work when it is employed to underpin narrative inquiry (see Chapter Four).

Goodson & Sikes (2001) suggest that life history research take one step further, '(b)y providing contextual data, the life stories can be seen in the light of changing patterns of time and space in testimony and action, a social construction' (p.18). Therefore, after Becker (1970), Goodson & Sikes conclude that life history forms a 'linkage in a chain of social transmission, a strand of complicated collective life in social and historical continuity' (*ibid.*).

Life history is essentially a collaborative and reciprocal process of developing understanding. The starting point is sharing research aspirations in ways that seek to empower the participants. Part of the research aspiration is the co-construction of meaning with the participants. The research can be more like a process where people come together to find out about/understand their lives and why they are so lived. Goodson & Sikes (2001) write that life historians invite their collaborators to consider and articulate answers to the following questions:

> Who are you? What are you? Why are you? Why do you think, believe, do, make sense of the world and the things that happen to you, as you do? Why have these particular things happened to you? Why has your life taken the course that it has? Where is it likely to go? What is your total experience like in relation to the experiences of other people? What are the differences and similarities? How does your life articulate with those of others within the various social worlds you inhabit? (p. 1)

Their list of questions continues. Often these questions are what 'ordinary' people would ask themselves, and do not exclusively belong to life historians or sociologists. Therefore, we say that in life history research there can be a shared aspiration (between the life historian or social researcher and her participants) in their inquiry into human life, or aspects of it. Inevitably, these questions, when put to research participants, would be reflexively engaged with by the researcher herself. Therefore, she is not merely collecting stories about life from her 'informants' and then writing them down in order to represent them. Rather, the life historian and her personal life and her own stories become intimately connected with those of her research collaborators. We will look in more detail at the nature of narrative encounter in Chapter Five. Here we highlight briefly that this relationship ultimately brings about reciprocal learning by both the researcher and the researched, about their experience of the social world, and how the different social dynamics and cultural elements interact resulting in their individual and collective experience as such. Together with other testimonies and historical documentaries and data, the life history locates individuals' and groups' experience in wider contexts.

In this way, life history work provides an opportunity to re-examine social research by acknowledging the complexity of human encounters in the research process and integrating human subjectivity into it. Life history sensitises and locates an individual's lived experience within the broader social, political and cultural landscape of human history. The aspiration is to understand life within the historical and social context in which that life is lived. This is what makes it a life history rather than a life story.[2]

3. Challenges of doing life history work

Czarniawska (2004) points out that postmodernist thinking is found in the following three tenets within social research:

1. The rejection of the correspondence theory of truth.

2. Challenges to the operation of representation by revealing the difficulties involved in any attempt to represent something by something else.

3. Increased attention to language as a tool for reality construction rather than passively mirroring it (p. 12).

Agreeing that there is a 'crisis of representation', Plummer (2001, p. 13) suggests that there is a need for *'grounded, multiple and local studies of lives in all their rich flux and change'* (original italics). He proposes that individuals respond to it with a 'renewed passionate commitment to a self-reflexive, moral and political project in the human and social sciences' (*ibid.,* p. 14).

Life history as a qualitative social research methodology confronts the researchers with diverse challenges. The first and foremost challenge lies in the deeper epistemological and methodological domain. Goodson & Sikes (2001) suggest that the critical epistemological positions taken up by the researcher determine the research questions, data collection, analysis, interpretation and production of texts. This is a real challenge to many social researchers. Narrative research questions and even disrupts some of the researchers' long-held assumptions about truth and knowledge. The iterative nature of the research process implies an ongoing theoretical and conceptual reflection which can change the course of the analysis and interpretation, and even lead to a revision of the research questions.

Another challenge lies in the nature of the relationship between the life historian/researcher and the research participants. Hitchcock & Hughes (1995) highlighted empathy, collaboration, dialogue and intersubjectivity as important ingredients in this relationship. Muchmore (2002) discussed the 'friendship' between the researcher and the researched. Oakley (1981) explored 'reciprocity' in interview exchange, and Riessman (2005) describes the research relationship as intimate. Dominicé (2000) sees the researcher also as a guide during the participant's exploration of her experience. In all contexts, the researcher engages actively with the participants and connects closely with them both on a personal level and within the research domain. Hatch & Wisniewski (1995) go further to suggest that this relationship may proceed on the 'lover model' where the key commitments include mutual respect and trust. The authors maintain that the relationship is to be 'mutually beneficial'.

Following Kant, Muchmore (2002) suggests that the key to the research relationship is not to instrumentalise. In other words, to respect the participants and not perceive them as the means to an end, even when this end is to understand their experience. Indeed, reciprocally sharing personal experiences and self-disclosure may be necessary for building bridges in research relationships and ought not to be suppressed (Measor & Sikes, 1992). We will return to this point when we discuss the challenge of research ethics.

Related to the above is the challenge involved in the presentation and re-presentation of narrative accounts. Hatch & Wisniewski (1995) continue to suggest that authorship, ownership, and voice are issues that concern the participants as much as the researcher. They ask: 'Who speaks for whom and with what authority? Whose story is it? Who owns the products of the work? Who is the author? What are the purposes of life-history taking?' (*ibid.*). Hatch & Wisniewski also contemplate how to work through issues of knowledge, power, control and privacy, in particular, that giving voice is not to 'underscore our perceptions of those with whom we conduct research as disempowered' (*ibid.*).

Amongst the concerns the for representation of narrative accounts, Bar-On (1993) points out that there is the possibility of the research process and the resulting publication harming the participants, causing pain and other distress to themselves, their families and their communities.

Many authors maintain that one of the major challenges with life histories lies in the difficulty the research design has to achieve both representativeness and generalisation. This challenge is connected to the ongoing concern for validity in analysing individual stories as the basis for understanding groups and mass experience. Does the inquiry into individual lives provide opportunities for a deeper understanding and meaning which can be significant for us all? On this some authors offer insights, in particular, that there is not a huge difference between generalising understanding drawn from the stories of individuals and that from mass phenomena, if that is an appropriate term. Here we offer an extended quote from

Thomas & Znaniecki (1918–1920) to provide fuller elaboration of the issue:

> In analyzing the experience and attitude of an individual, we always reach data and elementary facts which are exclusively limited to the individual's personality, but can be treated as mere incidences of more or less general classes of data or fact, and can thus be used for the determination of laws of social becoming. Whether we draw our material for sociological analysis from detailed life records of concrete individuals or from the observation of mass phenomena, the problems of sociological analysis are the same, but when we are searching for abstract laws, life histories as complete as possible constitute the perfect type of sociological material, and if social science has to use other materials at all, it is only because of the practical difficulty of obtaining at the moment a sufficient number of such records to cover the totality of sociological problems, and of the enormous amount of work demanded for an adequate analysis of all the personal materials necessary to characterize the life of a social group. If we are forced to use mass phenomena as materials, or any kind of happenings taken without regard to the life histories of the individuals who participated, it is a defect not an advantage, of our present sociological method (pp.1831–1833).

Hatch & Wisniewski (1995) also acknowledge the same challenge but sees it as a matter of

> balancing the story of the individual in all of its uniqueness with the larger social, political, economic contexts which frame it, and are, in turn, reinforced and challenged by the individual's action and responses (p. 120).

They raise the question:

> How do we place the individual within her social context and demonstrate the powers and forces that shape her experience and also provide a rich description of her story, her shaping of the world? (*ibid.*).

In this way, the challenge is not merely wrestling with the tension between the individual and the social but also a question of structure and agency.

Finally and perhaps most importantly, is the ethical challenge that confronts both life historians and their participants. This challenge is strong and enduring (Riessman, 2005). It might be suggested that there are no strict rules and prescriptions for ethical conduct in life histories and ethnographies (Guba & Lincoln, 1994). Researchers are not necessarily aware of the possible impact life history research can have on their participants (Hatch & Wisniewski, 1995). Thus research ethics confront the life historians on an ongoing basis due to both the nature of the research relationships as examined above and also the processes that the researcher and the participant go through together. Research ethics are indeed situated and contingent to the research context (Plummer, 2001).

Muchmore (2002) explains that there is a blurred boundary between what is ethical and what is not, and dilemmas, which can be complex, often arise within the context of the research. What is considered ethical in one situation may be perceived as unethical in another. Muchmore further points out that there are problems with the different ethical domains of life history research. For instance, informed consent poses the question of consent to what? Often in life history research, the participants are unaware that they are giving consent for another person to come into their lives and take a close look at them. It also begs the question of how far the participant can understand and anticipate the kind of risks and benefits of a process-based and contextualised commitment. Hence Josselson (1995, pp. xii/xiii) suggests that:

> Merely waving flags about confidentiality and anonymity is a superficial, unthoughtful response. And the concept of *informed consent* is a bit oxymoronic, given that participants can, at the outset, have only the vaguest idea of what they might be consenting to. Doing this work, then, requires that we find a way to encompass contradictions and make our peace with them.

Gill (2005, 2007a) argues that life history research can be an intervention and interruption in the participant's life. Because of the centrality of life narrative to the individual's self-identity, and the temporal orientation of narrative construction (in particular, in enabling a person to identify the direction of future actions), life history work inescapably provides opportunities for change (in the participants and the researcher) that otherwise would not necessarily take place.

However, Goodson (1995) and Sikes, Nixon, & Carr (2003) both warn that life history research's claim to be empowering and emancipatory for the participants is not necessarily robust and to a certain extent might be 'naïve' and 'ethically dubious' (Goodson & Sikes, 2001, p. 99). These authors are more concerned with the possibility of disempowerment and with overly exaggerated claims of emancipation and empowerment.

Nevertheless, this warning does not exclude the general possibility that as a result, narrative, life history and biographical work can be therapeutic. There are fundamental differences between life history interviews and therapeutic interventions, where the latter have clear guidelines for clinical practice to protect both the therapist's role and the patient's privacy (Bar-on, 1993). Therefore not having clear and strict rules for life history interviews will continue to pose ethical challenges to the researcher and her participants despite all the potential benefits and outcomes mentioned above.

In some ways life history work involves inevitable border crossing into therapy, into other social sciences, into broad humanistic inquiry and concerns. This is inevitable when the material under study is the messy subjectivity which comprises human being-ness. By staying true to the subjective forms, life history is therefore both iconoclastic and in process. This is not a methodology that can be painstakingly proceduralised, because for the subject of study is not amenable to such approaches.

Instead of broad principles and prescriptive guidelines, Riessman (2005) calls for 'ethics-in-context' to negotiate the 'give and take' of research relationships in life history and narrative work. She writes that the researcher's emotions are 'highly relevant to the conversations about ethics because emotions do moral work: they embody judgements about value' (p. 473) and that both the researcher and the participants in the (research) dialogue 'have subjectivities and emotional lives that they bring to research relationships' (p. 476). For that reason research ethics must consider the individuals involved as emotional beings with uncertainty and anxiety; and conflict and frustration can arise as a result of the interactions between these emotional beings. Emotions as a challenge further add to the complexity of the constantly negotiable and questionable power dynamics of life history research.

Goodson & Sikes (2001) indeed point out that the effects of any research on the participants and the researcher can vary from 'insignificant' to 'life altering', and from 'idiosyncratic and local' to 'global'. It is risky but rewarding at the same time. We will elaborate on this further in Chapter Three, which examines the process of life history research.

4. The use of life narratives in different disciplines

Narratives as research process and data are found in different disciplines. There has been growing interest in this approach for research into health. Atkinson (1997) examines the narrative turn and argues that sociologists, anthropologists, and others are paying increasing attention to the collection and analysis of personal narratives as a way of understanding health. This has led to an increased use of stories in qualitative health research, where narratives of suffering and illness have been granted special status. In the meantime, Atkinson offers a criticism of research in which narratives are regarded as offering the analyst privileged access to personal experience.

Connected to this is the use of narratives in therapeutic encounters, such as those in the disciplines of nursing, social care, gerontology, psychology, counseling, adult education and creative therapies (Bornat, 2002; Gergen, 1996). These disciplines are grouped together because therapeutic use is characterised and determined by the way the interviewee/participant/patient/learner sees him/herself through their stories and thus defines their lives accordingly. This process challenges the assumptions and embedded patterns in a person's life and relationships, which then leads to renewed stories and a transformed sense of self.

Narratives as research data are also found in studies of life writing (Jolly, 2001). This includes an amalgam of autobiographical material such as autobiographies, biographies, diaries, oral histories, blogs, reality television, photography, letters, documentaries, graphic memoirs, exhibitions, mobile phone texts. These narratives are not necessarily always collected by a researcher; rather more often than not, these narratives are shared amongst two or more persons, or a group of people.

Reminiscence work is used to collect the life histories of older people. It takes the form of guided autobiography—a short, or mini, autobiography, with one person guiding another through the telling of his or her story in his or her own words (Birren & Cochran, 2001). Guided autobiography is a generic and global term that is used here to include reminiscence (see R. Butler, 1963). It also features the use of a variety of multi-sensory triggers to stimulate shared conversations on an agreed topic or theme relating loosely to the known background and interests of older participants (Gibson, 1994).

Life history approaches are widely used in the study of teachers' lives (Goodson, 1991; Cortazzi, 1992; Hargreaves & Goodson, 1996b; Beattie, 2003; Day, 2004) and in teachers' thinking and personal and professional development (Carter, 1993; Casey, 1995; Clandinin & Connelly, 2000; Cole & Knowles, 2000, 2001; Connelly & Clandinin, 1990; Elbaz, 1990; Goodson, 1992a; Witherell & Noddings, 1991). One strand of this approach is using life history in teacher education by exploring teachers' autobiographies, learning biographies and other forms of life writing (Dominicé, 2000; Gill, 2007a; Karpiak, 2003; Day & Leitch, 2001)

In recent years, narratives and life histories can also be found in the work of conflict transformation and peace building. They offer an opportunity for the inner workings of transitional processes to be revealed to individuals and communities who have suffered from violence. Truth and reconciliation processes such as those in Latin America, South Africa, Rwanda and Sierra Leone are examples of how the exchange of life narratives between victims and perpetrators can lead to forgiveness and reconciliation (Gobodo-Madikizela, 2003; Gobodo-Madikizela & Van Der Merwe, 2009). We will revisit this last genre of work in Chapter Eight.

Questions for discussion

In the recent period of postmodernity our understandings of research processes have moved beyond the positivist and objectivist pursuit. The search for meaning and data has focused more commonly on subjective appropriation and interpretation. The narrative turn and rehabilitation of life history reflect this embrace of subjectivity. What has been called the 'Valhalla of voice', 'the Nirvana of narrative' marks an important shift in our understanding. But, as with all new directions, there are costs and benefits.

In this chapter we have tried to show how life history studies provide a particular response to the narrative turn. We have argued that it is a research methodology particularly suited to the renewed emphasis on subjectivity that accompanies the increased interests in contextualised meaning. At the same time we have pinpointed the methodological and ethical dilemmas confronting life history work. These exists because life history work focuses squarely on the human condition in all its complexity and variability. It engages the researchers and social scientists in bravely addressing issues such as emotional responses, political choices, and moral visions and more. So far from seeing this as a methodological problem, in this book, we see it as a supreme virtue.

In the next chapter, we detail the process of life history research. The following are a few questions that can help prepare a further review and reflection on researcher positionality:

- What are the main impulses and influences behind the recent 'narrative turn'?
- Why is it that narrative and life history work cannot be proceduralised?
- Do you think there are differences between narrative inquiries and life history work as illustrated in this chapter? Why or why not?
- What are the main challenges and concerns for those undertaking life history research?
- Does life history work involve particular ethical dilemmas or does it simply make overt that which is normally covert?

Further reading

Becker, H. (1970). *Sociological work, method and substance.* London: Allen Lane.

Bertaux, D. (1981). *Biography and society, the life history approach in the social sciences.* Beverly Hills, CA: Sage.

Bulmer, M. (1984). *The Chicago school of sociology.* Chicago: University of Chicago Press.

Plummer, K. (1983). *Documents of life: An introduction to the problems and literature of a humanistic method.* London: Allen & Unwin.

Plummer, K. (2001). *Documents of life 2: An invitation to a critical humanism* (2nd ed.). London: Sage.

Personal Narratives Group. (1989). '*Truths*' *in interpreting women's lives.* Bloomington, IN: Indiana University Press.

Tierney, W. (1998). Life history's history: Subjects foretold. *Qualitative Inquiry,* Vol. 4, No. 1, pp. 49-70.

3

Understanding the Life History Research Process

There is an elaborate disciplinary apparatus for condensing and recon-
stituting . . . narratives. This apparatus is premised on a particular kind
of relationship between researchers and people and things studied.
Research is a way of imposing order on an external world. . . . Narrative
accounts are reduced and inserted into the stream of representation and
are transformed within that network, into objects in a debate between
researchers from which the producers of the narrative are excluded.
—Jan Nespor & Lize Barber, 'Audience and the Politics of Narrative,'
in J. Amos Hatch & Richard Wisniewski, Life History
and Narrative, 1995

Introduction

In this book we aim to develop a deeper understanding of the process involved in life history and narrative research. This understanding is fundamental to our further developing the idea of narrative learning and narrative pedagogy.

We believe that life history research ought to honour and respect the narrative of the life storyteller first and foremost and, at the same time, be open to opportunities for dialogic encounter and collaborative interpretation between the researcher/listener and the teller. In this chapter, we take a closer look at the life history interview encounter, the establishment of research relationships, the process of analysing narrative accounts and narrative exchanges, as well as the construction of a life history. This allows us to go deeper and try to understand the nature of the narrative encounter, relationships, and how life history research impacts on both the participant and the researcher.

In order to avoid this outline of life history research process seeming context-free, we draw our insights from the research projects we have engaged in over time, amongst which are the recent example of the ESRC 'Learning Lives' project of which Ivor was one of the research directors, and Scherto's longitudinal research into the overseas Chinese students' journey of studying abroad and returning to settle back in China. These research projects help illustrate how we designed the research and engaged in the challenges embedded in the different stages of life history research.

Towards the end of the chapter, we offer a narrative profile which captures the changes over time as the participants engaged in dialogic interchange with the researcher and other research participants.

1. Overall life history research process

Although life history cannot be definitively proceduralised it is sensible to characterise the main stages in the process of life history construction. Often, life narratives are collected through a series of in-depth interviews. Working from this starting point, any interview encounter is inevitably overlaid by issues of power and stratification. Researchers can either work to engage with these issues or by ignoring such matters, serve to obscure or exacerbate them. The following sections set out in a somewhat painstaking manner to explain our own experiences with regard to the research process and interview interaction. The intention is to engage the reader in our examination of the life history research process.

Selecting research participants

The first consideration in life narrative interviews is often the selection of research participants. In the Learning Lives project, the researchers were concerned to provide a wide spectrum of participants and conducted an informal survey to establish a cross-section of possible participants in terms of age, gender and class (see Bruner, 1990; Halbwachs, 1980 for an argument to support this need for such a survey). The research team also conducted some 'pilot' interviews in order to establish a provisional spectrum of possible situations and themes to review. This was the start of a process of progressive 'strategic focussing' to identify and then explore the major themes emerging.

An issue that needs to be firmly confronted when selecting the participants is the selective bias in the choice of life storytellers. For instance, it is a common response of researchers to choose participants that appeal to their own instinctive storylines or the kind of life trajectories that the researcher sympathises with. This has now become a frequent complaint about life history research—the researchers are effectively telling their own stories. To avoid this, the Learning Lives research team tried, where possible, to act against this and chose a wide range of interview participants, particularly those who come within the cross-sections noted above and the themes delineated.

To further illustrate the importance of being aware of researcher bias, we refer here to an example from studies that Ivor was involved in some years ago—an investigation into teachers' life histories. Research into teachers' lives often brought to light the life histories of the more pioneering or innovative teachers. It is less common for the conformist or conservative teacher to be chosen in research accounts. There is a structural and locational reason for this, usually because the research interviewer was previously a teacher who moved into an academic position, and stories of his or her prior experiences as a teacher are often associated with those of a pioneer innovator. This autobiographical imperative sometimes leads the researcher to focus on teachers who have had similar experiences as non-conformists. The result can be a biased account which may overestimate the prospects for change and innovation in schools, where in effect, schools are often embedded in contextual inertia and such circumstances do not often favour the pioneering innovator (Goodson, 1995). To resolve this, Ivor and his team found it necessary to cover a spectrum of participating teachers from pioneering ones through to more conformist and conservative teachers.

Setting the scene for research interview and building trust

Having chosen the research participants, the next stage in developing life history research is what might be called 'setting the scene'. Strangely, often little thought is given to the background context in which the life history interview can be conducted, and yet it is of enormous importance. So often, only the researchers themselves are familiar with the methodology and the rationale behind the life history approach to the interview process, and such 'technical' details are seldom conveyed to the research participants.

We believe it is crucial for researchers to share their understanding and intentions with the participants. Sharing methodology not only empowers the participants to engage more actively in the research but also reinforces the participants' awareness of the importance of their own experiences and stories in the research and the significance of sharing and listening to each other's stories during the research interviews.

Setting the scene for the interview can be the key to the interaction. To give an example, in a recent life history workshop, two women who did not know each other decided to sit facing a picture throughout the interview rather than facing each other as a way of easing into the interview. The advantage of sitting side by side is that you can slowly turn to each other when you are ready to make eye contact instead of insisting on it from the beginning. If you insist upon it from the beginning, it often forces the situation which, to these two women, would have felt very unnatural. Laurence Stenhouse, an early English ethnographer, once argued that the best way to conduct interviews was by sitting alongside each other while driving a car. This way, the interviewee can look out of the window and only occasionally turn to make eye contact with the interviewer. Likewise the interviewee is free from the immediate interrogative eye of the interviewer. As if to confirm the point, it is a well-known fact recorded in a number of films and novels that taxi drivers elicit the most amazing confessions from the people who travel in their cabs and this is possibly because of the positioning of the two interlocutors, and the fact that they are never likely to meet again.

Nonetheless, the setting of the scene for the interview is a highly personal decision although one that has a great impact on the subsequent interview(s). It needs to be related very carefully to the next stage of the process, which is the building of trust. Building trust with the interviewee is an incredibly personal and complicated process. Trust has to be established if the interview is to be successfully conducted and for a reasonable interactive 'flow' to take place. In a sense, the speedy nature of the conventional research interview can be the problem. It is usually the case that the interviewer and the interviewee have to quickly bond with each other; come to some kind of agreement with regard to the interview process and rapidly develop some sense of intimacy and trust before there can be any meaningful exchange of views.

Life history research often requires more than one interview, which makes building trust an endeavour over a longer period than the 'speed dating' procedure described above would allow. There is no programmatic way of establishing this pattern of building trust. It is wholly a question of working with human chemistry and there is no procedural formula. What is clear, however, is that the more one explains the process and the use of the life history approach to the interviews, the more that in itself begins to build trust. In our own research, often during the first meeting, we, as the researchers, made a point of explaining the purpose of the interview, how it might proceed, and what was going to happen to the interview material when the interviews were completed. Often, this transaction was conducted around the signing of the informed consent protocol and the explanation of this protocol all came to be part of the process of building up trust.

The interview(s)

We see the interviews and thereafter the developing of a life history profile as a personal and intimate process from the beginning and believe that it needs to be based on a reciprocal interchange of views. Because we want the person's life story as experienced by him/her to be the central axis upon which the interview is based, our initial interviews tend to follow a particular pattern.

In the interview process, the aim is to encourage personal elaboration and 'flow' with minimal interrogation in the first instance. 'Flow' refers to the form an interview takes when the interviewees take off and begin to talk freely about their experiences, transitions, concerns and missions. It is easy when reading interview transcripts to establish when flow is taking place, but during the research, the flow has to be carefully encouraged.

For a start, there will be very few questions and the sections of interviewee's narration will be long, intense and meaningful. A peppering of interview questions can quite quickly break this flow, and we try to avoid doing this unless it is absolutely strategically and cognitively necessary. It is almost as if we, as the researchers, intend to keep a 'vow of silence' in the initial phases of the interview. This is not to say that the interviews are totally unstructured. There is often a narrative guide (usually consisting of the themes that emerged during the pilot interviews) used in two ways: first, as a 'fall-back' mechanism if the 'vow of silence' method does not work; secondly, even when the life storyteller is in full flow, there will be aspects of coverage which have not been fully explored.

The key is to give the participants the opportunity to be in overall control of the ordering and sequencing of their life stories. In return, this creates an appropriate context and space for 'flow' to occur. A major reason for us, as researchers, seeking to maximise the narrative flow of the life storyteller rather than directing or intervening in the initial process, is that it provides crucial clues as to the narrative character of the teller. Narrative character refers to the particular form and content of the life story (also see Chapter Four). It also provides some remission from the 'power' of the initiating interviewer/researcher (although we are cognisant that this can never be fully suppressed). The interviewer wants to unfold not only how the interviewee can respond to narrative probing, but also what past and existing narrative activity is going on as part of the person's lived experience. The breadth and depth of narrative activity help the researcher understand the degree of personal elaboration and construction that goes into creating narratives. To understand where on this spectrum of agency life storytellers are placed, it is then vitally important to let the teller sequence and develop her life story account in her own way.

Developing life history

Building on the initial life stories in the interview, a further dialogic interchange is developed. This is either a second interview or the later stages of an extended narrative exchange. There the two interlocutors, the interviewer and the interviewee, move more towards a 'grounded conversation' and away from the somewhat singular narrative of the initial life story telling. For us, this move to a grounded conversation is an extremely crucial move, for it signals the move from life story to life history, by which we mean the progressive understanding of the life story is being located within its historical contexts through collaborative interpretation and meaning-making, as well as triangulation by using other sources of testimonies, documentaries and historical data. This means approaching the questions we listed in Chapter Two but also inquiring into why stories are told in particular ways at particular historical moments in the life story to locate its meaning.

As we have already pointed out in Chapter Two, the distinction between life story and life history clarifies a major difference in the types of narrative research. Much work undertaken in the name of narrative research focuses on eliciting other people's stories. This objective becomes both the starting point but also the end point of the process. The narrative researcher becomes the sponsor or 'scribe'—eliciting, writing down and indeed, often publishing other people's stories. The approach is essentially passive and politically quietist. Little work can be done, of the kind described as using 'triangulation' in life history work. By contrast, life history work underlines the importance of placing the life narratives in their historical contexts, and there is a strong sense of research collaboration which helps locate each unique story in a broader frame—providing wider historical insights for the life storyteller and the broader audience for whom the story is recounted.

In summary, despite our rejecting a procedural approach to life history research, we have nevertheless emphasised a possible phased process, especially a move from life story narration stressing the agency of the teller, to a more collaborative grounded conversation where the interviewee and the interviewer seek further insights into the life story being told. Whilst conceptually and methodologically distinct, these phases often shade into one another with an overlapping period at which point the interviewer and the interviewee begin to probe and question the stories more actively and collaboratively.

This phased process moves us from life story 'narration' to life history 'collaboration' in our research. This is an absolutely crucial transition, not least because some narrative traditions remain locked in the first phase—namely the researchers 'collect' people stories and accept them as 'data'. The interpretation is often undertaken by the interviewer/researcher, working alone, at a subsequent stage. In this case, the *prima facie* evidence is the narrated life story. There is then, no second phase where life history is collaboratively generated. Collaboration involves employing other sources of data, such as other people's testimonies and a range of documents. This allows the interlocutors to historically locate the life narrative. In life history work, the interpretation and development of data are through the collaborative interpretation between the life storyteller and researcher.

To a great extent, life history interviews interrupt both the 'ongoing conversation' which underpins the life narration and aims to sponsor the dialogic encounter and further narrative meaning-making. This potentially leads to learning and transforming of the understanding of the interviewer and interviewee's life journeys as well as clarifying ways to engage in their future actions. We will expand on this in later chapters of this book.

Another pre-condition of life history work is the belief in human potential. By collaboratively interpreting personal narratives and 'locating' life stories as part of 'a chain of social transmissions', and understanding them in their historical context, the scene is set for the potential transformation of both interlocutors. To understand the historical conditions of a life as lived and of a life story as told is to comprehend that our world is socially constructed. Once the process of social construction is made more transparent through the collaboration, it becomes possible to think of new acts of social construction. Life history work then is both a reformulation of individual and collective memory and an ongoing development of 'social imagination'.

Social imagination is one of the most empowering and transformative modalities. *1984* by George Orwell tells how the collective understanding of history and social imagination are the twin evils that 'Big Brother' seeks to control. Hence work which sponsors collective memory and social imagination as narrative encounters can prefigure a transformative possibility. The life history exchange is then a place for imaginative narrative construction. As Czarniawarska (2004) says, a life history interview can 'become a micro-site of narrative production' (p. 51). Our view is that the activation of narrative production is an aspiration shared by both parties in narrative encounters. One task is the co-production of a story of action within a theory of context—a new narrative transformed by historical understanding and enhanced social imagination. As Brooks (1984) said:

> We live immersed in narrative, recounting and reassessing the meaning of our past actions, anticipating the outcome of our future projects, situating ourselves at the intersection of social stories not yet completed. (p. 3)

The life history encounter that works at the point of this intersection in a modality of exchange and sharing is based on reciprocity and trust. It involves then, the co-construction of meaning and a re-constitution of selfhood, as we have described. Thus life history represents a specific set of values and aspirations. According to Goodson (2003), it is a 'prefigurative practice'. A prefigurative practice is one that foreshadows and embodies the kind of world everyone would like to see exist more generally. It is set out in the microcosm of the encounter in order to make a pattern for relationships in an imagined ideal world. This world needs many ingredients to facilitate human development, and some of which are present in the narrative encounter.

As described here, life history work aspires to develop a dialogic exchange of views between the researcher and the participant(s). We are aware of the proactive stratified terrain on which this approach is played out and of the difficulties in re-working these expectations and structures. Nonetheless, life history interviews are a production location for the mutual exploration of meaning and selfhood. The life storyteller can be the expert par-excellence in the details of his/her life, and this sits well alongside the, no doubt, over-legitimised, expertise of the social researcher. Moreover, the initial life story interview insists that the interviewer listens very carefully. The encounter then builds on the expertise of the life storyteller. As the life story moves towards the life history, the encounter works to develop a theory of context or a 'genealogy of context' (Goodson 1992a) where both parties can exchange views, vernacular theories, patterns of explanation, and in doing so, arrive at a new understanding—mutually negotiated—of the social, cultural and historical 'location' of the narrative (Also see Gill, 2005; 2010).

In developing the life history together through a collaborative effort the very intimacy of the exchange can contribute to a pattern of trust and reciprocity in learning. All the most generative life history encounters have these characteristics at their basis. The facility to construct a fully grounded life history together can be seen as engaging in an educational endeavour. In this way, life history work involves a particular 'pedagogic encounter', as meaning and shifts in the sense of self are both constituted through learning. This is what we later term 'narrative pedagogy' but here we only refer to it from the angle of life history research.

2. Life history research as a site for narrative construction

Following the outlines of the life history research process and the process of co-constructing life histories, this chapter goes on to make an important point that when life history work is conducted solely on the story level, i.e., the researcher tends to begin and end the project by 'capturing' a people's life stories, the part that the researcher plays is essentially to act as the scribe of these stories and present them as the articulate and authentic voice of the people, for example, the teachers or whichever group is being interviewed. This could leave, for instance, the teachers and the teachers' consciousness exactly where they were at the start of the process and does not necessarily allow any ground for a learning conversation or a progressive reflexive understanding to emerge from the exchange between the two people (researcher and the life storyteller) who are talking together.

As we have already pointed out, in some narrative work the story approach starts and ends with narration. After narration, only the researcher, not both parties, goes away to interpret and make sense of the data or the stories collected and heard. The analysis and theorisation belong to the researcher and the academic world. The researcher has to take over the remaining process because in the life story approach, researchers feel it is their responsibility to continue the analytical and hermeneutical endeavour. So these researchers listen to these stories again and again, have them transcribed, read them in parallel to others' experiences, interpret and analyse them, and sieve through them in the light of existing theories. This appears to be the kind of systematic approach that any 'responsible' researcher would take. What the life story approach researchers do next is to hand the transcriptions over to the participants and ask: 'Do you agree with my reading of your life?' By this time, although it seems to be an empowering act, have these researchers effectively disempowered their participants by taking over a key part of the process?

Once the researchers put things into an academic framework, there is such perceived authority in what they produce that it immediately overpowers the participants. They look at the text and they don't understand how just one aspect of their personal stories has now acquired layers of interpretation and theorisation. They don't know how to relate to this project any more but are in awe of what the research has been able to do with their stories. Most participants might venture to disagree with part of the transcripts but rarely disagree with the interpretation or theorisation. It must be right, to their minds, as researchers are seen as people with powerful rationalising intellects. In this way, there is no equal partnership between the researcher and the researched from the outset. The researcher holds the power of knowledge, and acts as the knower, while the storyteller is overwhelmed by the power of academe and acts as the information provider.

What is described here is how life history research can, by contrast, be typically an intervention which involves conversation and narrative exchanges between two people engaging in a collaborative process of reflexivity and meaning-making. The interlocutors help each other in the development of their personal narrative. This potentially leads beyond the original story that is told, i.e., the starting consciousness of the storyteller to the interviewer and the storyteller engaging with new understandings, new data, new documentation, and new testimonies from themselves and from other people. The emerging narrative is the result of this exchange. In other words, the life history evolves when all the other bits of information have been fed into the progressive narrative development. Therefore, it is not just 'you tell me your story, I'll write it down'. In fact, the initial life story merely starts off the conversation but does not finish it. It is the encounter between the research collaborators and in the range of new perspectives brought to that ongoing encounter that an understanding of lived experiences evolves which goes beyond the original story itself.

In our studies of teachers' lives we have seen through the life history approach that recent teachers have been, in one sense, constructed by a training process. If we interview recently qualified teachers in the first years of their teaching experience, the stories they tell are primarily of teachers who are technically compliant with what a system of fixed curriculum, targets, testing and league tables wants them to do. By contrast, in life history interviews with teachers in the 1970s, they told completely different stories which were often stories about themselves as 'autonomous professionals' who could initiate all kinds of innovative practices within their own classrooms. The life history interview and the dialogic exchange can help the researcher and the teacher participants come to an understanding of why they, the teachers, tell particular stories in the way they do at particular times. Teachers thus become more aware of how teaching as a profession is politically and socially constructed.

Life history involves a collaboration through which data is developed in a prolonged reciprocal exchange—mutual interpretation and emerging theories are shared, discussed and 'tested'. In this way, understandings of the life narrative emerge in the course of the exchange, and interpretations are grounded in the dialogic encounter. Life narrative is therefore not static recitation but an evolving process of narrative re-construction, re-telling and becoming.

Goodson (2006, p. 18) argues that it is necessary to 'build in an understanding of the context, historical and social' in which human experience and learning take place. Therefore life history, at its best, aspires to be a narrative exchange between equals, two people searching together for meaning and understanding. The search is to 'locate' the selves within their respective stories and in their broader social and historical contexts.

3. Narrative as research intervention

This way of understanding life history research poses a huge challenge from the point of view of research ethics. The non-interventionist approach can make a researcher feel more comfortable as he/she does not aim to interrupt the participants' lives. All the researcher does is to allow the participants to share their lived experience or life stories, without necessarily leading to any further consequences. A social researcher who is conscious of research ethics will also be comforted that he/she is broadcasting the participants' voices as they are heard.

Indeed, this view of social research has a seductive appeal, including the intention to empower, to give a voice to the silenced and to access a wider audience, to transcribe, and to bridge the lived world with the intellectual world. However, as discussed earlier, momentary power is perhaps the most profoundly disempowering. That is the ultimate paradox.

Here we are arguing for something different: a more considered exchange of stories and a clearer sense of dialogic encounter. In moving from life story focussed narrative research to life history work we seek to change both the underpinning research methodology and the potential for reciprocal exchange.

What may also be derived from this is that whenever research elicits people's life narratives or uses them as a basis for understanding the social world, the researcher has to think about the methodology as well as the pedagogy of using life stories. The reason for including pedagogy is because all social research projects inevitably lead to some change in the participants' understanding after an engagement in the narrative process. The change can be on different levels, such as an individual's perception of the social world or their sense of self, ideas about the life that has been lived so far and how he/she might live his/her life in the future, and so forth. In a way, however the research ethics are defined and whatever steps are taken to protect the respondents, change happens. If it happens anyway, it is then necessary to reflect to what extent, as social researchers, we actually engage in the process.

This leads to the view that life history research is not just a narrative encounter; it is a pedagogic encounter. This aspect will be explored in more detail in later chapters, including an investigation into what kind of learning takes place during the narrative encounter.

Historically, the narrative turn aimed to help researchers move away from a positivist approach to a more holistic and interpretative approach to understanding the social world. There are other uses of narratives, as illustrated in Chapter Two. This suggests that there has been recognition of the importance of the human subject and human subjectivity, rather than studying people as objects. The complexity of narrative research and the various pitfalls embedded in it call for more mindful and careful thinking before launching into narrative and life history projects, especially as there is an ethical minefield out there. A set of discussions is necessary in order to prepare researchers for the complexity of social encounters. There is a need to sensitise the human encounter, but paramount is to understand more deeply the nature of such encounters. We will attempt to do this in the second part of the book.

The challenges embedded in life history research force researchers to accept that there is no way to completely suspend power relations and stratification and other issues in the world. It is just not possible. This kind of encounter forces the researcher and those being researched to confront these issues together in an open communication. That is the supreme virtue of this form of research process.

Therefore, trying to remain distant and objective and to leave the research subject's life intact is impossible. One claim is that narrative and life history research inevitably interrupts the participants' life by posing deep personal questions and offering opportunities for self-reflection (Gill, 2005). In this way, life history research starts with the person's narrative and ends with an examined account of life or lives in context.

Life history also offers another opportunity to re-examine the nature of social research in a more critical way, not only from the point of view of the complexity of social interaction and social dynamics that sociologists are already addressing, such as gender, power, race, class and so on, but also by opening up the complex inner landscape of a human being, of a person's emotions, subjectivity, identity and personhood. Endless ethical debates about life history research will remain, and so they should. Narrative work is fraught with ethical and emotional dilemmas and so is human life.

4. 'A bird in a cage'—Jasmine's narrative

Elsewhere, we have argued:

> The role of the narrative researcher is to facilitate and promote the voice of the participant, and often to present that voice unchanged, for fear of 'academic colonisation'. Indeed colonisation has been a real issue in social research. However,

forgoing all collaboration is, we would argue, a form of abdication. It can leave the teller or the participant with their story 'uncontaminated' but also unchanged. In other words, no further understanding is pursued (Gill & Goodson, 2010, 157–158).

In this section of the chapter, we want to use a case study to give an example of how research conversation can serve as an intervention and an opportunity for learning and the growth of the research participant.

Jasmine was one of ten students Scherto interviewed on a research project which investigated overseas Chinese postgraduate students' journey from China to study in the UK. Jasmine was twenty-two when the project started. The project interviews lasted for one year during which time Scherto met with the students for individual interviews at least once a term, and in a group of three or four once a term. There were many informal meetings in between where ideal opportunities were created for the group to share stories and for dialogic interchange.

The following is the edited narrative profile that Jasmine and Scherto co-constructed:

> When I was growing up, the majority of young people of my age in China came from one-child families. The media often says that these lone children were brought up as little 'emperors' and 'empresses', and were the centre of attention of their extended families.

But my life was nowhere like that of an empress.

> I was born into an intellectual family. My father is a university lecturer and my mother an editor and later an entrepreneur with her own publishing company. Both of my parents came from very humble backgrounds and had worked really hard to arrive at their positions. So working hard is their motto. In a large country such as China, most people have the same motto. I understand it very well and appreciate the kind of struggle people go through in order to avoid staying in poverty.

> As far as I can remember, I had always been kept under close parental control like *a bird in a cage*. This perhaps was due to the fact that my parents were in their late thirties when I arrived and they wanted to take good care of me. Still as a child, I really resented my parents' so-called protection and the fact that they made all the decisions for me simply because they know what is best.

> Growing up as a kept bird, at the same time, I was very much encouraged to explore the world of knowledge. I learned to read and write at an early age and have been a keen reader even since. I can still remember my childhood favourites

—the great Chinese masterpieces such as the Monkey King stories, the Legends of the Water Margin, stories of the Three Kingdoms, children's fairy tales by Hans Andersen and the brothers Grimm and tales from the Arabian Nights. These books encouraged my enthusiasm for reading, and created a world of fantasy. Books were my escape, books made me feel free.

Schooling, even primary school, was like torture—large classes, teaching was mainly drilling, and work was always so heavy. I never felt that I had any childhood. At school, we sang songs about childhood—oh sweet childhood, innocent childhood, joyous childhood full of discoveries and fantasies. But where was the sweetness, the innocence, the joy, the discoveries? My generation had none of these experiences as the children were turned into little studying machines in order to compete for limited opportunities to enter higher education.

The only real childhood I had was in those books, but even that didn't last long. The fantasy world had to give place to loads of homework every day. My parents removed all the 'unnecessary' books from my room, and replaced them with prep-books for exams. They kept saying that if I failed the exams I'd have no future. I must work hard and not be 'dreamy' because 'no one can pass the university entrance exam by simply dreaming'.

But I was dreaming. I dreamed of the day when I could be free, for instance, to leave home and to go to the university. There was no question that I'd be heading towards higher learning—one of my parents' expectations. For them, my future was a good school, a good university and a good job.

I had my own plans—I wanted to attend a university in order to be free from my parents. So I worked very hard and willingly in order to do well at the university entrance exams. I did excel and came up with good results. Then when it was my turn to choose the university to apply to, my parents suggested, no, they never suggested anything, they insisted that I attend a local university. It happened to be very prestigious—it ranked 5th in the country. You can't imagine my disappointment—*the bird failed to escape from the cage.*

University life wasn't too bad; at least I didn't have that much pressure from my parents to study hard. I also got to live on campus during the week, and reported back home at the weekend. I studied mass media and communication and found the subject really interesting.

At that time, many Chinese families were able to afford to pay for their children to study abroad. A number of students from my university were awarded scholarships to study in North America and in Europe. My heart took flight just imaging the freedom I would have to be so far away from my parents. Don't get me wrong, I do love them and appreciate their love and protection, but I also believed that they could love me in a different way, for instance, by trusting me to be capable of flying high without their help, or finding my own happiness.

My parents took my desire to study abroad as high aspiration and surprisingly they actually encouraged me. They wanted me to be part of the elite and were willing to financially support me to pursue an overseas study plan. So I took this opportunity and that was my escape route—*the bird finally flew from the cage.*

My first encounter with the West was love at first sight. With the help of Chinese students who had arrived earlier, I settled in England quickly. Despite many adjustment issues that I had to face such as cooking, shopping, adaptation to Western approaches to teaching and learning at the university, finding friendship amongst 'strangers', and being a stranger in a new place myself, living and studying in England and travelling in Europe was a time of tremendous growth for me.

I was aware of many changes in me—I was becoming independent in managing my personal life, but also becoming independent in my own thinking, which was most significant. What I loved most was to be able to make decisions for myself and know that these were good decisions. For instance, I chose to do an MA in Media Studies with an element of anthropology and then I studied a second MA in Cultural Anthropology because I was clear where my interests were and I was motivated to study. I also travelled a lot and when you travel, you have to make decisions constantly. These experiences gave me confidence in my own abilities.

In sharing a house with students from different parts of the world, I came across many different viewpoints about the meaning of life and about things of value. These different attitudes towards life, personal objectives and different ways of seeing one's place in the world have had a significant impact on me. I was truly inspired to take a fresher look at my perceptions and worldviews.

Being part of this research project and having such extended conversations with you and with other Chinese students on the project also helped bring many of my encounters and intercultural experience into focus, and made me more aware of cultural differences, and understand better why people think and do things so differently. Above all, I feel that I have now a better understanding of what it is to be Chinese. Before I left China, I looked up to the West, and thought everything Western was good and more interesting—Western education is better where children can play more and are happier, the environment is cleaner, there is more democracy, more human rights and more justice. . . . Don't we all think the grass is greener and moon brighter on the other side? Now I am more critical when thinking about these differences, but I am also more interested in seeing China with fresh eyes.

I am a changed person in many senses, and sometimes I say and do things in ways that surprise myself. I realise that I am also developing a new personality—I am more mature, open, less shy, and I am more, what is the word, indomitable, than I have ever known. I am more appreciative of my parents. They have also noticed the changes, and I don't think they are quite sure of what it all means when I return home.

I am ready to return. That is what I see as the essence of freedom. I have flown away from the cage where I felt captive, but now I can return with a sense of freedom because I have a stronger sense of myself. I am returning to the place where I grew up because I know there are things I want to do there and I think I can make a difference to the people whom I care about.

Many Chinese students want to stay in England or Europe for work experience with a view to settle, but I know that my work, my life and my place are in China. I want to produce TV documentaries that tell particular kinds of stories, the stories of *the forgotten, the abused, the vulnerable and the ordinary* and we all know that there are many of those stories in China. I want to tell these stories in ways that they can be heard by people who can help make changes. That will be my project, for now.

5. Dialogue and reflection

Ivor: Reading and re-reading Jasmine's narrative profile, I can really see that your research itself served as an intervention in a number of ways: first, the research interviews provided an ideal space for Jasmine to make sense of her lived experience growing up in China as a lone child. She has chosen a really interesting metaphor that captures well her journey into freedom. Second, the research brought together participants for dialogic exchange and shared meaning-making. It was clear from the text that she was developing new understanding about her own culture, for instance. Third, the research conversation and editing her own profile further gave her an opportunity to consolidate an emerging and stronger sense of herself. Let's just take a moment and review the process you went through to come to the text.

Scherto: This text was not the full transcript but rather a narrative profile and intended to be short. Jasmine turned twenty-four when we completed editing it. So nearly two years had gone past since the research first started. She revising the text to a certain extent to reflect her understanding over time.

The text was a collaborative effort. I put together the first draft after reading through the huge transcripts of three in-depth one-to-one interviews and conversations and many group discussions. Jasmine read the draft and keenly edited her own words. She said that this was making her narrative more retrospective and introspective. She deleted some text and added others. For instance, where she discussed the loss of childhood, there is only one line in her initial interviews. The paragraph was added afterwards as a result of a group conversation about the differences between schooling in Britain and in China. Lin, another participant in my research, was studying for her MA in Education Studies in the UK, and she shared with the group some of the debates currently being carried out in England about children's wellbeing and social and emotional development. Jasmine then had long passionate discussions with Lin and others about the lack of respect for children in China and the fact Chinese schooling system actually prevents children from enjoying learning, etc. Then we read the edited text, discussed and finalised it together.

Ivor: I can't help but feeling that there are several gaps where there is more to explore.

Scherto: You are right to say that there are gaps in Jasmine's narrative profile. In this excerpt, Jasmine's decision to work as a documentary maker reads somewhat out of context. The context was that as a media student and later a student of cultural anthropology, Jasmine noticed that China was becoming a hot topic for the Western media. But to her, too much emphasis was laid on the country's unprecedented economic growth, and not enough on understanding China as a whole and on the ordinary people's lives. The research provided a space for Jasmine to have conversations on this topic with other participants too. Jasmine felt frustrated by the fact that the gulf between the 'haves' and 'have-nots' is widening, and little is done to help the under-privileged. After being exposed to charity work and philanthropist work through her own volunteering during summer holidays, Jasmine became more aware of her own privileges and the suffering of those who live in poverty and desperation.

In one interview, Jasmine expressed immense compassion when she spoke about her experience in a Chinese hospital where her mother stayed for a week due to a minor operation. Jasmine saw the luxury of the private room her mother was in, which was in total contrast to the general ward, where more than twenty people were in the same room, and the chaos in the hospital corridors. She was compelled by her empathy and began to listen to these people's stories.

There were many other critical incidents where Jasmine explored the changes that she was experiencing in relation to herself and how our conversations helped her internalise such shifts. These were in the interview transcripts and could not be included in the profile sketch due to the limited space allowed.

Ivor: You mentioned Jasmine's emotional responses in the research conversations. How significant were emotions in your research interaction?

Scherto: In the narrative encounter, feelings and emotions were responded to with intense listening and feedback rather than judgment and opinions. Sharing in-depth personal stories allowed myself (the researcher) and the participants to focus on what stimulated emotional responses, and we worked together to reflect on and analyse these experiences.

Ivor: As a researcher, you are moving from an acquaintance relationship with the participants to friendship. This is a question about research ethics. Kenneth Plummer (2001) encourages all researchers to reflect on their own emotional selves, in particular, after spending a period of time with an individual or a group of individuals, and after listening to their stories intently as you did because there is an 'active emotional re-engagement', in Plummer's words.

Scherto: Indeed, Plummer suggests that the researcher may even 'fall in love' with the participants. Therefore it is necessary for researchers to be more reflexive about the emerging relationships in the research. Certainly through this research, friendships grew and I was close to all the participants, and remain friends with at least two of them. What comforted me was this shared meaning-making in a group and the opportunity for the participants to co-construct the texts of their narrative profiles. I felt that I wasn't exploiting the 'informants' by interrupting the flow of their lived experience, then going away and making a thesis out of their generosity. Instead, the research was a deep reflection and learning for all. Such profound sharing and intense listening created bonds between us in ways that only close friendship could have done.

Questions for discussion

In this chapter, whilst illustrating the process of life history research, we also made a point that the life history should aim to provide 'a story of action within a theory of context'. In examining work employing life stories and narratives, it is essential to consider the balance between 'stories of action' and historical and social 'theories of context'.

In the above discussion we have argued that many narrative methods focus on people's stories, especially their stories of action. Little attempt has been made to develop theories of context.

- Take a narrative research study and examine the balance in the text between people's 'stories' and the development of a 'theory of context'.
- Take time to see how the researcher developed the theory of context if any, especially what other sources of data were being employed and how they were used.
- If the research begins and ends with stories, is this because the aim is to 'capture the person's story' and/or is it because of the nature of the research method employed?
- Scrutinising a narrative research study also involves assessing the aims of the researcher and evaluating the nature of the research collaboration. How does the collaboration (if any) affect the original life story told?

In this chapter, we reiterated that life history work tends to advocate a collaborative approach to understanding narrative and that the researcher and her participant(s) move into the interpretive phase together within the domain of the research questions and life stories shared. The aim is to collaborate over stories of action but also to develop emerging theories of context.

- How practical is it to seek to develop narratives and theories of context collaboratively? Is it too time consuming?

- Do emerging themes and theories of context allow researchers and participants to develop a broader sociological, historical, and even philosophical understanding through life history work?
- How do issues of power and the 'academic division of labour' intrude onto the process and how can they be dealt with?
- Examine your own experience in the field. What are the sources of expertise and disciplinary criteria employed in your research interpretation? Does the research process change the understandings of the interviewee or merely record existing understandings? In what way does the research process change your own understanding in terms of both the research question and yourself as a person?

Both the narrative and life history methods enter into the complex web of human subjectivity and perception. This moves such research into a domain of great ambivalence, nuance, uncertainty and even chaos. When compared with the narrow certainties of more positivist methods, this makes such research time-consuming and demanding.

- Is the time involved and complexity of the undertaking proportional to the understanding developed? Is a full immersion into participants' narratives and life histories necessary to develop a full understanding of human subjectivity?
- Some researchers have applied mixed-method approaches to the studies of people's narratives. Compare the strengths and weaknesses of the full immersion approach and mixed-method approach.

Further Reading

Chamberlayne, P., Bornat, J., & Wengraf, T. (Eds.). (2000). *The turn to biographical methods in social science: Comparative issues and examples.* London: Routledge.

Fraser, H. (2004). Doing narrative research: Analyzing personal stories line by line. *Qualitative Social Work, 3,* 179–201.

Goodson, I. (2003). *Professional knowledge/professional lives.* London & New York: Open University Press.

Halbwachs, M. (1980). *The collective memory.* F. Dulles & V. Ditter (Trans.). New York: Harper & Row.

Mishler, E. (1986). *Research interviewing: Context and narrative.* Cambridge, MA: Harvard University Press.

Roth, W. (ed.) (2005). *Auto/biography and auto/ethnography: Praxis of research methods.* Taipei: Sense.

4

Narrative Construction and Narrative Capacity

Now a whole is that which has a beginning, a middle, and an end. A beginning is that which does not necessarily come after something else, although something else exists or comes about after it. An end, on the contrary, is that which naturally follows something else either as a necessary or as a usual consequence, and is not itself followed by anything. A middle is that which follows something else, and is itself followed by something. Thus well-constructed plots must neither begin nor end in a haphazard way, but must conform to the pattern I have been describing.
. . .
Furthermore, whatever is beautiful, whether it be a living creature or an object made up of various parts, must necessarily not only have its parts properly ordered, but also be of an appropriate size, for beauty is bound up with size and order.
. . .
To give a simple definition, a length which, as a matter either of probability or of necessity, allows of a change from misery to happiness or from happiness to misery is the proper limit of length to be observed.

Aristotle, The Poetics

Introduction

In Chapter Three, we touched upon the notion of individual narrative character. In this chapter we explore in more detail in what ways a person's narrative character may be a vehicle or a hindrance in his or her narrative meaning-making. A deeper understanding of the narrative character can also serve as the basis for our emerging discussion on life history research as a pedagogic site for learning. This pedagogic site allows researchers to seek more opportunities during the narrative encounter for fruitful engagement and conversation leading to a potential for transformation in the perceptions of each individual, their relationship with others and their actions in the social world.

Below, we first review Labov's work on the structure of personal narratives. Then we draw on recent research experience to examine the different narrative characters observed and analyse how these impacted on the participants' potential for deeper understanding and learning during the life history research encounter.

The example of Christopher below shows there is the possibility to shift the narrative character during the life history interview depending on the way the research collaborators engage with each other and the participant's willingness to re-construct the narrative.

Finally, we draw attention to the potential pedagogic points which might be helpful to encourage learning during the narrative encounter. In this process, we try and unpack the notions of 'pedagogic site', 'learning' and 'moral' action.

1. Narrative characteristics

Narrative characteristics were first identified by Labov (1972) who suggested there is a correlation between social characteristics and the structure of a person's narrative. He put forward a model of narrative structure with six categories which refer to the narrator's way of explaining an event in her life:

(1) *Abstract* is a brief summary of the gist of the event/story. It draws the audience's attention to the story that the narrator is about to tell.

(2) *Orientation* is a further explanation to set the scene: when and where the event/story took place and who or what were involved and so on.

(3) *Complication* is the core of the event/story giving details of 'what happened' and is sequentially ordered in time

(4) *Resolution* recapitulates the key moment of the event/story.

(5) *Evaluation* is to make the point of the story clearer to the audience.

(6) *Coda* is a generalised statement to signal the end of the story and stress the point that the narrator is making.

According to Labov (1997), this model helps the researcher/interviewer to have a reliable means of recognising the process of development and the ends of stories. At the same time, sociolinguists have become increasingly interested in the ways that individuals narrate their lived experiences, especially how they elaborate their stories by using particular linguistic characteristics and by drawing on other linguistic resources. Together these also allow social researchers to understand how individuals tell stories of gender, ethnicity, class, age, or concerning particular professions or vocations. Through this model, social researchers can become sensitive to the fact that storytellers or narrators tend to shift their narrative characteristics depending on the choices they make, the sources of self they are speaking from and the contexts within which they are speaking.

However, Labov's model cannot be easily used for the emplotment of the narrative sought in the life history research discussed so far in this book, especially the kind of relationship between narrative quality and the potential for shifts in understanding. In particular, we are interested in the kind of shift in the understanding of oneself, others, the social world and historical contexts within which each life unfolds and how individuals might reformulate their course of action in accordance with the new understanding. Our own research experience has taken us on a journey where we began to witness some emerging narrative patterns of individuals when they narrate their lives.

This particular work was undertaken by Ivor Goodson and colleagues in the ESRC 'Learning Lives' project that took place between 2004 and 2009 (Goodson et al., 2010; Biesta & Tedder, 2006). At the beginning of the Learning Lives project, the researchers shared a commonly held assumption: whilst all stories are different in substance since everyone is a unique human being, these stories would share recognisable and common aspirations and forms. In other words, everyone tells stories, narrates their lives and the structure of the narration ought to be broadly similar. However, this common assumption proved to be false. Through interviews with over 120 participants, the researchers observed that not only are stories different in substance, but there are distinct and recognisable differences in the basic structure and aspirations of stories.

This means that each individual's personal response is distinct according to his/her style of narration—narrative 'character'. Each person's specific interpretive mechanisms process these experiences based on very distinctive and broadly recognisable patterns. As we all reflect on our stories we need not only to find our story but understand the distinctive manner in which we interpret, recount, employ and perform it. This interpretative process is what we call narrativity, and it is a vital ingredient of who we are and of how individual narrative characters differ from person to person. It may partly help explain how people respond differently to the same event and how their moral, civic and political stances vary accordingly.

In the Learning Lives project, the demography of the life storytellers covered a wide range, from the young to the old, from the homeless to the privileged, from the unemployed to creative artists. However, unlike Labov's model, the initial social labels provided little guidance to people's narrativity. Whilst there are links between social position and styles of storytelling, this is in no way determinist. Narrativity, in short, allows a variety of interpretative responses to social position and social structures. Moreover, since storytelling is often linked to personal plans and aspirations, these provide a variable interpretive mechanism when confronted by social forces. This is not to say social forces are not crucially important, but it cannot be assumed there is a direct relationship between social patterns and individual responses. Any strategy for social improvement needs to work both with social patterns and narrative responses because they are interlinked in their effect on human subjectivity and motivation.

Since the project lasted over a period of four years, people were observed interpreting new events at different stages in their lives course. An identifiable process of interpretation and subsequent narration often seemed to be at work. It was possible to see to a degree how people's life stories were adapted, added to, altered and sometimes quite substantially transformed.

In brief, an individual's narrativity or their narrative character may have impact on their learning potential and actions. Narrating and constructing narrative forms an important part of a learning process of transforming understanding. In this way the emplotment can signify the narrative strategy of the life storyteller as it allows the narrator/author to depart from established norms and patterns of belief (Bruner, 1990).

Some of the insights from the Learning Lives project relate to the different identifiable patterns of narrativity. People have different kinds of 'narrative intensity' which Goodson (2006) defines as the length of the initial life story that the narrator tells and the amount of detail and depth such an account offers. By and large, individuals can be locked into a continuous narrative flow when they have high internal reflection and an ongoing internal conversations (also see Biesta & Tedder, 2006). Conversely, when that internal narrative activity is, for whatever reason, less frequent, it is more difficult to achieve narrative flow in the life history interview. The interview process is highly contingent on the narrative intensity of each participant, which in turn, depends—to a considerable extent—on the degree of internal reflective activity, as well as the relationship and trust established during the research. *Xr intra personal ia*

Goodson, Biesta, Tedder, & Adair (2010) have grouped the different narrative strategies that individuals apply in narrating their lives into two broad categories: descriptive and analytical or evaluative. After revisiting and analysing some of the conversations and narratives in the Learning Lives project and through our own research dialogue and conversations, we further expanded on our understanding of the possible narrative characters of the individuals interviewed and summarised this understanding in the figure/model that we developed below. Before we go into details, we would like to add a note of caution—despite the fact we tried to illustrate the different narrative capacities by devising a visual representation, this is by no means to suggest a fixed way of interpreting the differences in the narrative characters, nor do we intend to put in place or imply any fixed patterns or categories.

High narrative intensity refers to those people who seem to live 'in the narration' or have spent a good deal of their time reflecting upon and fine-tuning their stories. Those with high narrative intensity can come under two categories: 'A' type narratives tend to be detailed, finely tuned but also reflective. When interacting with people with more elaborated but also highly analytical narratives during the research, the interviewer would sense they were privy to an ongoing internal 'conversation' in a constant process of becoming. Another way of explaining this is that narrators in this category tend to employ narrative construction as a central mechanism in their meaning-making.

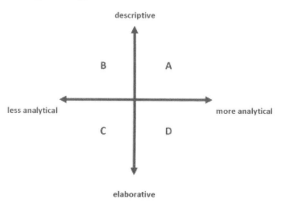

Figure 1: The spectrum of narrative character

In contrast, although narratives in the 'B' category are also from those who have high narrative intensity, they are less reflective and less analytical. The narrators may appear to enter a narrative flow easily and often their stories proceed in a well-rehearsed and largely unprompted manner. Sometimes, highly elaborated and less reflective narrators can tell what we call a highly scripted story. Here scripted narrative refers to accounts that are elaborated according to a particular version of life. Narratives in this category can bear the kind of social linguistic characteristics identified by Labov. These are socially provided scripts: 'I am a farmer, I'll die a farmer.' as one interviewee said in the Learning Life project. For the researchers of the project, there is strong evidence that such minimal personal elaboration and reflection resulted in a limited exercise of agency or learning.

At the same time, it also emerged that individual narrative capacity is deeply rooted in culture and social forces including gender, ethnicity, race, class, profession and so forth. For some, the scripted narrative is open to re-construction, and for others, it is fixed in a strong version of his/her life and may prevent the narrator from engaging in a different account and hence may hinder any learning or new action. Later, in Chapter Six, we will take a closer look at how a narrative might shift during the interchanges and encounters we described earlier.

'C' and 'D' both refer to less elaborated accounts. With less narrative intensity, however, the interviewer seemed to have more difficulty in eliciting the life stories. Since the life story is less actively reflected upon and rehearsed, there is less narrative flow to connect with. Often the interviewer witnessed a more hesitant process of narrative construction. It is true that not all people are practised narrators or practised internal narrative constructors. Yet the life stories are often there, present, while perhaps less accessible. It is not so much a question of narrative presence or absence, more a question of the intensity with which the narrative is reflected upon, rehearsed and recounted. This is often the case with those whose narrative qualities are within category D.

This pattern of personal narrative elaboration is closely linked to the issue of emplotment—something hinted at in the quote from Aristotle at the beginning of this chapter. Narrative quality can be assessed by the sophistication of the emplotment of the life narrative. The development of a course of action is linked closely to the elaboration of a 'plot', or emplotment. In some ways emplotment then links the sponsoring of personal agency to the on-going development of learning strategies. The progressive refinement of the 'plots' in life narratives illustrates the enhancement of narrative quality and the opening of the narrative to action and to learning trajectories. We will return to this in the next chapter.

Let us re-state this spectrum of narrative quality. We should like to stress that differences in narrative quality do not lead to a hierarchy of esteem or efficiency but serve as an aid in the understanding of the different patterns present.

The spectrum covers what we have called more 'scripted' narratives at one end and more elaborate and reflective/analytical narratives at the other. It shows that narrative work can shift between being a somewhat passive process, a retrospective recounting of what has happened to the narrators and a transformative encounter with others and above all, with the other of oneself such as in the case of Jasmine's narrative. This can be a process of re-authoring or re-constructing the narrative. This could be linked to the delineation of a distinctive 'course of action' as we shall see in the example given below where we examine the source of the narrator's identity project and personal agency.

However, highly elaborated narratives which work with a higher degree of personal crafting do not necessarily always result in learning and better understanding and agency.

2. Christopher's narrative on his learning in and from life

Christopher is a puppeteer, born in 1942, in the south of England where he has lived most of his life. His natural parents split up when he was two years old and shortly after, his mother remarried, so that Christopher was brought up by his mother, who became an alcoholic and agoraphobic, and his stepfather with whom he has not been able to build a 'father-son' relationship. Christopher is homosexual and this, along with coming from a broken home, seems to be central to his understanding of his life story.

From very early in his life, Christopher recalls, he felt that he was marked out as a 'traveller', an 'eccentric' who did not quite match the labels often given to people. From around the age of eight, Christopher immersed himself in the world of puppetry.

He went to school, and later to art school to study theatre design. Theatre design was a compromise with his parents who wanted a 'safe' career for Christopher and would, perhaps, have preferred that he enter the family business designing battery covers. During his time in formal education, including at art school, he was, as he says, 'sleepwalking' through much of his education. What inspired him was learning as much as he could about what he needed to know to become a successful puppeteer. This was becoming his 'life project': puppetry. He gained an apprenticeship with a renowned master in puppetry and left college without completing his theatre design course.

From then on, his life and learning were to revolve around his development as a puppeteer. As well as formal learning opportunities, Christopher also learned through immersion with experienced puppeteers.

Early on, Christopher entered into a relationship with a man who was to open up for him whole areas of the world of art that Christopher had not been aware of. When the sexual relationship waned, they were to remain friends, and, perhaps 'learning partners' for many years, until recently when the friendship was broken off and is missed greatly by Christopher.

Towards the end of the interviews in 2008 Christopher's sexual partner of 28 years had left him, and Christopher found himself at a crossroads in his social life at a time when he felt his creative work had reached an important 'watershed' or 'epiphany'. Within his work he has attained a 'stage' where he incorporates aspects of his being into his work, so that he and the puppet show are intertwined.

This was also the first time he had confronted mortality. As a new part of his life unfolds in his social life, so Christopher hopes he will be able to resolve the inner/outer world struggle he feels present through this difficult phase of his life, in ways that are creative, for as he says, 'that's the learning'.

Yet throughout his relationship difficulties, what remains central to Christopher is his work as a puppeteer and his desire to intertwine his 'vocation' with his spiritual, or inner needs, and his work on his self-project.

3. Self-understanding and transformation through narrative

We explore the research interview process or dialogue between Christopher and the researchers. Christopher had identified learning in this project in terms of his understanding of himself and the possible direction he will take in his future life. The analysis was drawn from discussions with Christopher, focusing on his narrative pattern and character, and although it may sound psychoanalytical, it is nevertheless not intended to be.

Christopher initially offered an extremely elaborated and almost well-rehearsed version of narrative—the child from a broken home (a mother who drank, a distant father), a homosexual who didn't fit the mainstream 'labels' and a puppeteer who could escape to a world where he was in total control and where he thrived in art and self-expression. The quintessential world that Christopher can control is the world of puppet-making and puppeteering. He had learned to distrust other people's emotional responses to him. The puppeteer environment consists of a set of wooden symbolic objects that he could control—literally. He said very clearly in many interviews that he will not lose control as he will never let anybody do to him again what his parents did to him, injure and hurt him in such a way. Being the puppeteer was entirely about creating the control and symbolic order which replicates humanity in some way.

For the first few interviews, Christopher's narrative account follows the same pattern—well elaborated, well-rehearsed and well-told. He is an excellent storyteller and each incident recounted further illustrates his main emplotment—early childhood trauma, feeling of alienation, escaping into the world of puppetry where he feels unthreatened and in control.

Yet towards the later stage of the dialogic exchange, Christopher was able to see a new part of his personal life, especially his social life, unfolding. For the researchers, it highlighted a two-stage ecology—finding balance and harmony between one's inner and outer world. The first stage was when the internal narrative took him to the place where he has a holistic sense of what he might be—namely a puppeteer. He said that he could see that it had stabilised his working life, and was a helpful response to his early trauma; his mother being a very heavy drinker, his birth father leaving home without warning, and having no real relationship with his stepfather. That is why, perhaps, Christopher said that he had that awful sense of loss which he brought into his world and why he was able to comfort himself through his original narrative of the puppeteer.

However, when the Learning Lives project took place and the interviewers met Christopher, he was just over 60 years of age and coming out of a long term personal relationship. It was a time of great hiatus in his life, because as well as changes in his personal relationships and his relationship to work, his relationship to mortality was also changing. So these were part of what he brought to the narrative encounter. The project went on over a period of three and a half years and the narrative exchange became part of the fabric that made up his life. Christopher said that he looked forward to the 'interview' day, and the researchers looked forward to seeing him too, a very reciprocal response to the narrative exchange.

In those three and a half years, Christopher was moving into a different narrative character. His original story or his original solution to a lot of his dilemmas was that he would cluster a narrative around himself as a puppeteer and commit himself to work and locate himself within the puppet studio most of the time. His work identity always took priority over his relationships. However, the research project prompted him to question his own narrative elaboration to such an extent that he said: 'For the first time in my life I am willing to throw the pieces up in the air and just let them fall.' Christopher was, in a sense, willing to give up on the whole pattern of control which had given him a work identity and allow the deconstruction of that kind of self to take its own course. This is what the researchers considered a second part of the ecology because it enabled him to uncouple from his early narrative as a resolution to an original trauma and begin to look in a differ-

y at that story, allow it to implode and a new sense of self to emerge. To 'throw the pieces in the air and let them fall' signifies a new kind of freedom and a detachment from his old trauma. This is what we call a new kind of holistic eco-logical moment.

Christopher's initial narrative character showed that it was about a person who is relatively controlled and disciplined. His earlier insistence on a well-rehearsed story confirmed his intention to be in control. Now he appears to be happy to say 'Well, maybe I won't be that, maybe I'll be something entirely different, I'm not sure what.' This seems to be a much more yielding, detached and ironic kind of position to be in. It is more ecological in the sense that for the first time, he real-ly accepts his own place in the cosmos.

The fact that these interview conversations took place at a time when Christopher's life was going through transitions might have impacted on his chang-ing narrative pattern. Mortality is on the horizon, and he speaks very cogently about it and admits that it is the first time that he has really thought about death. Accordingly, there seems to be a relationship between the impending sense of end and the freedom to actually be himself for the first time, such as giving himself per-mission to be whatever he now is.

So now a less controlled narrative emerged in the face of mortality. Thus Christopher was able to decouple himself from the original narrative settlement into something much more holistic and transformative. The account Christopher gives of taking responsibility for his own life and facing mortality represent the move towards what we call 'integrity'. We discuss this in greater detail in Chapter Seven (for a full discussion of Christopher's life history see Goodson, et al, 2010).

 Narratives have that epicentral function. They are more than just constructs, or illusions; they can also be concrete daily acts. That is the power of narrative sto-rytelling. It is as central as that to understanding the way human beings conduct themselves in the world.

4. Dialogue and reflection

Scherto: In these two chapters, we explored how life history research can provide a dialogic and reflective space where individuals use nar-ratives to come to understand who they are and what determines their life's trajectories. In Jasmine's case, her narrative construction involves a clear project which is to help the under-privileged in China. In Christopher's case, it was an open text, a symbol of a changed narrative character.

Since in the second part of the book, we will continue to examine the relationship between dialogic encounter in a narrative exchange and individual's actions in the social world, I wonder if we could begin to explore from the two case studies these connections. Whilst both cases stressed the important of research dialogue and interaction, I am also interested in the narrative which not only emerges out of an on-going dialogue with oneself and with researchers and other participants, but also with those people whom one cares about. In Jasmine's words, these are the people from home. In fact, she was referring to people living in poor rural areas where her parents and grandparents came from. Her decision to embark on a project in order to make a difference for these people does not come from a free-floating moral position.

What Charles Taylor (1989) calls the 'web of interlocutors', or tribal folks in your words, can occupy a large space in the construction of a person's narrative. As you often say, some people remain in dialogue with you even though they have physically ceased to be, such as your dad, your Aunt Viv and your Uncle Clive. The community has an abiding power on a person and his/her narratives are intricately connected to these people.

The question to explore is whether narrative thus constructed through the dialogue with one's community is limiting or liberating?

Ivor: I believe that they are both. Narratives are Janus faced—they point both ways, they limit and, at the same time, liberate. Every narrative must have these qualities simultaneously. A person can be imprisoned within a particular (scripted) narrative and also be freed by it. The question is how to deal with the Janus-facedness of narratives. The local specific concrete ties to holding onto a vision of life are implicated in one's sense of oneself and therefore can be limiting, as we see in Christopher's early stories. These can be liberating in particular in the way of making a link between our concrete, specific, rooted sense of ourselves and a broader understanding of the human condition and universal values.

All narratives carry moral messages in one way or the other and images of the moral world. I think for me, the potency in narrative is partially linked with one's judgements about how values are embedded in the telling itself. When I make decisions in the world I literally and quite honestly 'talk' to my mum and dad and aunts and uncles nearly all of who are dead, and I ask myself 'What would Dad, what would Uncle Clive, what would Auntie Viv think if I did this?' So it's literally communicating with my ancestors who are the community that I am part of and who offer that commanding voice in my moral career and who are my moral compass. I have realised that my own personal hinterland is still very closely connected to a set of tribal folks that are important to me. That has never ceased to be true, and it has not ceased to be true since they have all died. I still talk a lot to them. So, all I'm saying is narrative is cast out of an on-going dialogue with a set of people the narrator cares about and it's not just a free-floating moral position. Of course, in my case, coming from a working class background, my moral position is related to broad humanistic views about oppression and dispossession and disadvantaged groups, but it's compromised in my case by having dialogue with the people I have known about these issues. So I literally give voice to these questions about how to behave in the social world by saying: 'Look, if I did that, if I actually join that gentleman's club, or went and did that, what would my Dad think?'

Scherto: I hear you are saying that asking our community moral questions can be a concrete example of a much wider set of interrogations one might have about the social order. One perceives the social order through the eyes of one's folks and one's community. Is that right?

Ivor: Yes, the two things sit perfectly well together for me. Having a community of voices to dialogue with doesn't mean that I dislike people who are not from my tribe. There are good human beings across the social spectrum. But there are a set of concrete moral questions that I want to address in the world. It's what I came to do—to pose specific questions learnt from my tribe out there in the world. So, for me, I don't see a specific narrative, a specific moral narrative, as limiting. I don't think it can be actually, if it's underpinned by universal moral concern. Similarly, I don't see that specifically interrogating yourself through your ancestors at a particular time is likely to limit you. If you ask me: 'Ivor, are you imprisoned within a vision of yourself as a working class hero?' I obviously would not want to believe that and I do think I am at the stage, not unlike Christopher, since I became 50 at least, where my own narrative is in one sense loosely coupled and more autonomous. Then, why am I still talking to my Auntie Viv and Uncle Clive and Dad when they're dead? I believe that for me, there is a specific historical moment of a specific set of class relations I am addressing here. It is not only specific but also has enduring moral implications for me. Those questions about oppression and dispossession are timeless questions, in my view, and actually probably more important now than ever. It was interesting to see that Jasmine, brought up in a typical middle-class family, would get in touch with the commanding voice of her parents' roots and her grandparents' roots. My guess is that she was more inspired by a universal moral concern as well as her own compassionate nature.

When people go through those gears in terms of their own learning, when they begin to understand that they are part of the common stream of humanity, that their dilemmas are, in fact, general dilemmas confronting everyone, and they can connect therefore to bigger meta-narratives and bigger concerns, that's when they move out of the prison of selfhood into a broader plateau of concerns—and that's learning, very profound learning.

Scherto: Is it right to say that your moral concern about the dispossessed, disenfranchised, and the oppressed has become what is underpinning your greater responsibility for being in the world—through your work, and through your writing, and so on? In order to support those people who are silenced by a particular social order, you are constantly giving voice to them. Your habit of thinking and habit of being is deeply situated in your tribal roots, perhaps deliberately and necessarily, in order to remind yourself of this greater responsibility you carry. In this sense, you have chosen to embed your selfhood in a particular narrative construct, rather than being imprisoned by it. By doing so, you are able to carry a very strong sense of moral duty within you. Can we also say that because you have such a profound commitment to the dispossessed, you carry with you a particular image that you want the world to see in you—a true 'hero' rising from the community that has been 'othered' by a political system? Is the working class hero image connected to your sense of personal fulfilment, to be the living counter-narrative in the mainstream discourse?

Ivor: It is more complex than that, I think. Finding a personal plateau of happiness and fulfilment and self-acceptance and acceptance of others and the world, that has again a Janus face because it can mean that one has a sense of wellbeing because one is reasonably well resourced and happy in the world—which I am. I mean, with a reasonably well-fulfilled family and personal relations—which I have. It could be that such contentment and such fulfilment leads to a deconstruction of that wider mission. So, I am personally happy, I am personally affluent, I am personally fine and personally and psychologically I am in reasonable order. So personally, the business is kind of done and dusted, but that's not the point. The point is having got to that stage, you are faced with a dilemma: I have now become privileged and affluent and joined the very social force that has oppressed the community I came from. I want to remind myself of my own roots by talking constantly to my ancestors and reminding myself of the endless pattern of disadvantage, of dispossession. I don't want my own personal sense of fulfilment to erode my wider sense of mission. That's what it comes down to.

I remember once you asked me: 'Why do you hold onto this kind of image of yourself?' It is for that very clear reason. I am absolutely clear about it. I am detached enough to know that's what I'm doing and I see no reason on earth not to do that because that is the moral place I want to be. It is what I came to say in the world. It's what I came to do.

Questions for discussion

In this chapter, we presented a finding from the Learning Lives project with regard to the individual's narrative characters. We suggested that they can cover a spectrum of categories from those that are mostly externally 'scripted' through to those that are more personally elaborated, more self-scripted, and to those that are highly analytical and reflective. Personal narratives, then, can have very different qualities, and the issue of 'narrative quality' is central to our understanding of narrative potential for personhood and agency.

These questions offer an opportunity for us to review our own understanding in the light of our experience in the field:

- Have you noticed any patterns in the narrative and life history interviews that you have conducted? How about stories that are gendered, classed, and narratives that belong to a particular profession or occupation, such as teachers or artist? Have you noticed any particular characteristics in these different groups' narratives?
- What is the significance of the narrative intensity exhibited?
- What is the relationship, in any, between narrative intensity and the delineation of courses of action or learning trajectories?

- What are the differences between narratives as 'closed' and those that resemble 'open' texts?

We believe that the question of whether a narrative is 'closed' or 'open' is of vital significance. When a narrative is closed the central script seems pre-determined and therefore somewhat determining of future actions. The person seeks new strategies with which to continue the script but the narrative identity changes very little. The scripted narrative provides a lynchpin core identity and allows new strategies to operationalise within that script. In substantial transitional moments, one scripted narrative may be exchanged for another scripted narrative—one 'farmer' for instance, moved on to become an 'engineer' and the new identity was adopted as a fully formed narrative identity, externally available and accepted as socially defined. So scripted narrators can adopt new strategies and in certain transitions adopt new scripts.

With open narratives there is considerable change at the point of transition. The person is practised in narrative elaboration and emplotment and is able to respond flexibly to new transitions. But the very notion of openness can lead to constant narrative elaboration and the absence of an established script and clearly defined course of action. Some elaboration leads to a sense of vocational or moral purpose and some does not. Some elaboration becomes almost an end in itself; other elaboration leads to a solid vocational, spiritual or existential project.

Such complexity requires us to reflect on questions such as the following:

- What is the relationship between narrative capacity, reflection and agency?
- Is narrative elaboration a gateway, a necessary precursor to formality, a personalised life mission?

Dr. Rowan Williams, the Archbishop of Canterbury, has recently stated in his afterword to the Good Childhood report:

> The truth is that when human beings act out their individual feelings without reflection or scrutiny, they are likely very soon to become incapable of living with each other (Lyard & Dunn, 2009, Afterword, p. 3).

Further reading

Andrews, M. (1991). *Lifetimes of commitment*. Cambridge, UK: Cambridge University Press.
Brooks, P. (1984) *Reading for the plot: Design and intention in narrative*. Cambridge, MA, & London: Harvard University Press.

Bruner, J. (1986). *Actual minds, possible worlds.* Cambridge, MA: Harvard University Press.

Daiute, C., & Lightfoot, C. (Eds.). (2004). *Narrative analysis. Studying the development of individuals in society.* Thousand Oaks, CA: Sage.

Goodson, I. (Forthcoming). *Developing narrative theory.* London & New York: Routledge.

Sarup, M. (1996). *Identity, culture and the postmodern world.* Athens, GA: University of Georgia Press.

Wolcott, H. (1994). *Transforming qualitative research: Description, analysis and interpretation.* Thousand Oaks, CA: Sage.

Part II: Narrative as Pedagogy

5

The Nature
of Narrative Encounter

But what happens when he (psychoanalyst) uses the same kind of reflection in a situation in which he is not a doctor but a partner in a game? Then he will fall out of his social role! A game partner who is always "seeing through" his game partner, who does not take seriously what they are standing for, is a spoil sport whom one shuns. The emancipator power of reflection claimed by the psychoanalyst is a special rather than general function of reflection and must be given its boundaries through the societal context and consciousness, within which the analyst and also his patient are on even terms with everybody else. This is something that hermeneutical reflection teaches us: that social community, with all its tensions and disruptions, ever and ever again leads back to a common area of social understanding through which it exists.
  Hans-Georg Gadamer, *Philosophical Hermeneutics*, 1977, pp. 41–42

Introduction

Part II of this book intends to move from life history work and narrative research to focus on examining those situations where life narratives are processes of developing understanding and learning. This helps us to systematically address the major issues that are crucial for establishing a theory of narrative pedagogy.

In this chapter, we focus on investigating narrative understanding within the hermeneutic framework. This can help us further examine, from a conceptual perspective, the nature of the dialogic encounters described in Chapters Three and Four and how they may lead to a transformed understanding within life history research. As discussed, to a certain extent the life history research process creates a pre-figured space whereby, through a hermeneutic dialogue and narrative encounter, individuals are given the opportunity to 're-configure' their own understanding of self, other, and the world.

We draw on philosophers such as Gadamer and Dewey amongst others to explore this process and how new understanding can be developed.

1. Narrative understanding—the hermeneutical project

Narrative understanding, it has been argued, is a hermeneutical project at the heart of which lies transformative potential through engaging in the process of narrative encounter. It has been characterised as a 'dialogue with the world' (through language) that gives rise to and shapes the individual's meaning and understanding of diverse human experiences. In this dialogic exchange, the personality and characteristics of the storyteller, his/her socio-cultural backgrounds as well as historical and ideological 'horizon', and the communities to which he/she belongs can 'support or constrain' understanding (Freeman, 2007).

In *Truth and Methods* (first published in 1960, but here reference is made to the 1989 edition), Gadamer argues that there are four main characteristics of the hermeneutic approach. These are summarised by Kolak & Thomson (2005, pp. 337–338) as follows:

First, it applies to things that have some kind of intentionality, even derivatively. This means that there can be interpretations or hermeneutics of social practices, people's experiences, texts, stories, paintings, but no hermeneutics of atoms, weather patterns, or galaxies.

Second, interpretation is usually contrasted with the logical positivist idea that applies in the methodology of natural sciences. The hermeneutic tradition is a methodology applied in the social sciences in order to understand the content or meaning of intentional states and human or social actions.

Third, interpretation is holistic in that to understand is to also to understand a web of interrelated meanings embedded in the concepts and contexts of the thing to be understood.

Fourth, interpretation is inherently historical, and when people seek to understand anything, it is necessary to employ concepts, ideas, and presuppositions that form a part of their historical tradition.

According to Gadamer, understanding starts from projection. Individuals project meaning for the text or narratives in our case, as a whole as soon as they think that they have grasped some initial meaning emerging from the text or the stories. The person who is reading the text or listening to the stories has particular expectations with regard to a certain meaning. This initial projection (fore-projection) is the pre-figuration which is constantly revised or re-configured as both the author or teller, and the reader or the listener continue to penetrate the meaning throughout the encounter.

Gadamer summarises this as follows:

> every revision of the fore-projection is capable of projecting before itself a new projection of meaning; rival projects can emerge side by side until it becomes clearer what the unity of meaning is; interpretation begins with fore-conceptions that are replaced by more suitable ones. This constant process of new projection constitutes the moment of understanding and interpretation (Gadamer, 1989, p. 269).

In attempting to understand, there is often a tension between the listener's existing understanding and the emerging meaning, which is also the difference between what she is accustomed to and what she is confronted with by the narrator. Gadamer suggests that generally, individuals try and resolve such tensions after 'the experience of being pulled up short' by the text, or the narrative. When the meaning in the text is 'not compatible with what we had expected', it 'brings us up short' and allows us to engage with it differently (*ibid.*).

Gadamer contends that whilst listeners engage with the meaning in others' stories or texts, it is impossible to 'stick blindly' to their own fore-meaning or prefigured ideas of the meaning of the thing that they, the listener, want to understand. The only thing to do is ensure that 'we remain open to the meaning of the other person', but this openness 'always includes our situating the other meaning in relation to the whole of our own meanings or ourselves in relation to it' (p. 271). According to Gadamer, in order to pay attention to the meaning implicit in a person's narrative, and achieve understanding (rather than misunderstanding), the criterion of questioning is very important. In this way, the hermeneutical task '*becomes of itself a questioning of things* and is always in part so defined' (*ibid.*, original italics).

Understanding involves encountering 'the alien'

For us, a narrative encounter encompasses a situation in which, when the narrator begins, the listener is prepared for the stories to tell her something. This is what Gadamer terms the 'foregrounding and appropriation of one's own fore-meanings and prejudices' (*ibid.*). In other words, the condition necessary for understanding is a sensitivity and an awareness of one's own bias as a listener, without which the story cannot present itself in all its otherness and hence loses the potential for understanding.

Historical consciousness as well as individuals' ontological schemes and worldviews is important to their understanding. The real thrust of the hermeneutical problem is thus, according to Gadamer, that all understanding involves some prejudice. Prejudice, defined by Gadamer, is 'a judgement that is rendered before all the elements that determine a situation have been finally examined' (p. 273). Instead of placing prejudice under a negative light, he suggests that it is 'where we can start' to engage with otherness. Gadamer writes in his book *Philosophical Hermeneutics:*

> Prejudices are not necessary unjustified and erroneous, so that they inevitably distort truth. In fact, the historicity of our existence entails that prejudices, in the literal sense of the word, constitute the initial directedness of our whole ability to experience. Prejudices are biases of our openness to the world. They are simply conditions whereby we experience something—whereby what we encounter says something to us (1977, p. 9).

He points out that being situated within traditions and prejudice does not necessarily limit our freedom. He asks: 'Is not, rather, all human existence, even the freest, limited and qualified in various ways?' (p. 277), and concludes: '*That is why the prejudices of the individual, far more than his judgements, constitute the historical reality of his being*' (p. 278, original italics).

In order for there to be understanding, one must not be aware of one's own prejudices, but also there is the pre-requisite of an encounter with the unfamiliar, 'the alien'. That is to say, understanding begins when we, as human beings, are prompted by strangeness. Therefore, the hermeneutic task attempts to resolve the dissonance in the experience of the unknown. Through our own familiar and common understanding, it is possible for everyone to venture into the unknown, the alien, and thereby broaden our horizons and our experience of the world.

The hermeneutic circle for understanding involves the interplay between the parts and the whole, and the harmony of the parts with the whole pertains to hermeneutic understanding. This is what Gadamer calls the 'hermeneutical rule', i.e., 'we must understand the whole in terms of the detail and the detail in terms of the whole' (p. 291). This may also be described as follows: the words of the narrator make up the total context of the story, and the story belongs in the context of the narrator's tales, and the latter in the whole context of her world. Meanwhile, the story, as an artefact and manifestation of her lived experience, belongs to the whole of the person's inner life. In this way, Gadamer concludes, the hermeneutic circle of understanding is not formal in nature, nor is it subjective or objective. In this way,

> (t)he anticipation of meaning that governs our understanding . . . is not an act of subjectivity, but proceeds from the commonality that binds us to the tradition . . . (which) we produce. . . inasmuch as we understand, and participate in (its) evolution' and it further determines our understanding (p. 293).

Understanding as the fusion of horizons

Gadamer points out the finite determinancy of human thought and suggests that the way the individual's own range of vision can be expanded is through understanding. He describes this vision by using the concept of the horizon, as follows:

> The horizon is the range of vision that includes everything that can be seen from a particular vantage point. Applying this to the thinking mind, we speak of narrowness of horizon, of the possible expansion of horizon, of the opening up of new horizons . . . (p. 301).

Thus, the horizon is not closed, it is rather 'something into which we move and that moves with us' (p. 303). Gadamer referred to horizon in the context of the historical past, but we could also perceive it from the position of a person, his/her own past, and the history and tradition within which he/she lives and where the horizon stems from. To take a step further, Gadamer saw that understanding occurs when a person encounters his or her past and the tradition or the history from which he/she comes and becomes. Gadamer summarised it thus:

> There is no more an isolated horizon of the present in itself than there are historical horizons which have to be acquired. Hence the horizon of the present cannot be formed without the past . . . *understanding is always the fusion of these horizons supposedly existing by themselves* (p. 305).

Accordingly, in a situation of life history research conversation where understanding involves the tension between the individuals' (narrator and interviewer) prejudices, it is essential to imagine the situation of the other person in order to get to know him or her and their stories. In other words, in a conversational or narrative exchange, the listener tries to discover the other's viewpoints and horizon. This in turn requires the listener to have a good knowledge of his/her own standpoints and horizon. Discovering the other's horizon is through 'transposing' to the other's position, which is not just by empathy, or by subordination; it is neither self-relatedness nor acknowledging and respecting the other; it is both. Eventually, as the listener continues to encounter something new in the other, there is a fusion into 'something of living value' (*ibid.*).

The nature of narrative encounter

We can understand the nature of the encounter based on our review of Gadamer's philosophical hermeneutics in four major inter-connected aspects[1]:

1. encounter requires attentiveness to the other, and otherness

2. encounter unfolds something new about the other, but also about the 'other' or the 'unfamiliar' of oneself

3. encounter has embedded in it the interplay of social and historical traditions

4. encounter involves different language(s) i.e. different modes of expression which play a part in enabling the fusion of horizon.

Encountering something new is an opportunity for enhanced understanding and meaning-making. This is because the interlocutors (in a life history research context, the interlocutors are the researcher and the participant; in a learning context, the facilitator/educator and the learner) are engaged in the ongoing flow of events, stories, and accounts of people's actions. There are countless moves, transitions, contradictions, anticipations, constraints, surprises, nuances of meaning and so on, which animate the dialogic exchange and give it an ever-emerging character. So encountering is an interplay which presupposes a prior context, or contexts, of assumptions, attributions, capabilities and so forth. To enter into the space of an encounter requires both the interviewer and interviewee, or the educator and the learner to be critically alert participants instead of critically detached observers or objective analysts. It requires attentiveness to the other, and otherness. It is also necessary for the interlocutors to be fully present and interact with each other as equal partners in the dialogic encounter.

Encounter as perceived in philosophical hermeneutics can facilitate learning in two ways: by offering something new (what Gadamer terms as 'alien') about what the person is attempting to understand; at the same time, unfolding something new about the persons engaged in the encounter. Previously undetected biases and prejudices, uninterpreted and un-negotiated meaning, as well as new insights, might thus progressively unfold about both the person and about what 'speaks' to the person regarding their efforts and their life's goals. This unfolding can be surprising, disquieting, challenging or inspiring.

In any case, the narrative approach to meaning-making and learning can be viewed not only as a matter of strengthening one's command of new stories or new interpretations of lived experiences but also developing new understanding of self, contexts, relationships with others and with the wider world: hence direction and mission in life can be consolidated. This new understanding or new perspective is the 'third voice', the result of the fusion of horizons which is the voice of dialogic collaboration. According to Myerhoff (1992), this is where two points of view or two perspectives converge to examine one life, one narrative. The third voice grows out of listening relationship (to which we will return in Chapter Seven). In life history research, the third voice could be (in the text) co-developed between the researcher and the participants; in educational narrative sharing, it could be the new understanding derived or new courses of action identified. The interlocutors here are at the same time listener and narrator. Myerhoff extends the notion of third voice to a third person—confirming a transformation of one's selfhood.

Within the narrative encounter is the larger social interplay and historical flow of that which is being discussed and explored. An awareness of this helps us to engage in the possibilities presented in the encounter. According to Gadamer, the real significance of any tradition, or more precisely, any particular embodiment of a tradition, lies in the claim to truth of an unfamiliar kind which it presents to the dialogue partners. In this way, the encounter is not primarily an event of transmission and acquiescence. Rather it is 'interplay ever-pregnant with possibilities of new understandings, confrontations, misunderstandings, transformations', and so on (Hogan, 2000).

As we discussed earlier a genuine encounter involves a 'fusion of horizons'. On the one hand is the horizon of understanding that the person brings with her to the encounter and, on the other, the horizon within the tradition which addresses her in this encounter. 'Fusion' is not a melting together in which all tensions are laid to rest but an attentive to-and-fro between the person and the otherness of that which addresses him/her. It is an interplay in which tensions are uncovered and brought to the fore rather than glossed over.

In this interplay a particular embodiment of a tradition, for example; social, historical, scientific, literary or religious, etc., is brought to active articulation, but that articulation and its own presuppositions can also be questioned and re-questioned by the person. In this way, he/she becomes in this event a more fluent and more discerning participant, as distinct from an 'expert' or an 'authority' on anything. The 'fusion' is itself an active seeking for a more inclusive and self-critical understanding.

It is primarily in and through language that human experience of the world gets expressed and understood. Gadamer describes language as the medium in which substantive understanding and agreement take place between two people. Language is key to dialogue and key to self-understanding in the encounter. Gadamer writes:

> In speaking with each other we constantly pass over into the thought world of the other person; we engage him, and he engages us. So we adapt ourselves to each other in a preliminary way until the game of giving and taking—the real dialogue—begins. It cannot be denied that in an actual dialogue of this kind something of the character of accident, favor, and surprise—and in the end, of buoyancy, indeed, of elevation . . . is present. and surely the elevation of the dialogue will not be experienced as a loss of self-possession, but rather as an *enrichment* of our self, but without us thereby becoming aware of ourselves (1977, p. 57)

According to Gadamer, to speak a language as one's own is to 'become a participant in an informal apprenticeship, where a growing fluency in expressions and turns of phrase is inseparably linked to certain opinions and convictions rather than others' (Hogan, 2000). Man is always encompassed by the language that is our own and in fact, 'in all our knowledge of ourselves and in all knowledge of the world' (Gadamer, 1977, p. 62). This is in line with Wittgenstein's thinking that language is understood not as a set of tools to be mastered and then employed at will, but as something which remains ever active in shaping our thinking and doing as well as our speaking. The effects of history, it turns out, pervade language and its usage just as thoroughly as they influence the consciousness, or rationality, of individuals. When a dialogue partner encounters an entire system of thinking, and the history behind it that is different from his/her own, new opportunities for learning are created. In addition, language conditions human experience and shapes the whole inheritance of understanding and learning. Our language conditions our thoughts and articulation and at the same time imprisons us. Encountering a different mode of expression in the language opens up channels for broadening our horizons.

From reading Gadamer, Crapanzano (1990) suggests there are many kinds of encounter in the narrative process, and 'how we respond to them depends upon our own assumptions about the significance of the encounter, the meaning of language, and the nature of understanding' (p. 274). According to Crapanzano, dialogue is rooted in Greek 'dialogos', meaning a speech or thoughts across, between, through two people. It is a passing through and a going apart at the same time. Crapanzano saw that there is both a transformational dimension to dialogue and an oppositional one. Narrative encounter is a process of creating a new understanding through dialogue, an understanding of the differences between the horizons each person brings to the dialogue which could be 'indeterminately far apart, in all sorts of different ways, when they started out in their conversation' (Tetlock, 1983, quoted in Crapanzano, 1999, p. 270).

In summary, the narrative encounter is also a confrontation with one's own past, lived experience, assumptions, values and meaning scheme (Mezirow, 1990), the culture and community of 'web of interlocutors' that have contributed to our identity (Taylor, 1989), and the beliefs and rationales that underpin the decisions we have made in terms of how to live our life.

2. Emotions in the narrative encounter

Narrative encounter involves people meeting and experiencing each other on many intertwined levels; in social relations, personal inter-relationships, the mental, emotional, physical and the spiritual. It also takes place at the level of personal dispositions, beliefs, values, goals, commitment and aspirations. This whole-person aspect has been often neglected in understanding narrative research. It is usually considered a cognitive exercise drawing on both the socio-historical contexts of the event and the individual's subjective account of the meaning of the event and experience. Most life history projects have been conducted in this manner.

There is a potential limit to narrative and life history work if the interlocutors/collaborators are not engaged in the process of narrative encounter as whole persons, or in other words, both parties must engage in the narrative process as who they are (and who they were and who they are to become) with their emotions, intuitions, thoughts, cognitive capacities and dispositions. This might resemble the kind of relationship that Carl Rogers described in his person-centred counselling.

In this limited space, three aspects of narrative encounter are considered: the relationship between rationality and emotion; the role of emotions in narrative encounter; and encountering each other as whole-persons in the narrative processes.

Rationality and emotion

The earlier discussion in this chapter appears to locate the hermeneutic approach to narrative in the light of a rational analytical framework. However, there is increasing acceptance and growing literature on the association between cognition and emotion, and acknowledgment that emotion is the driving force behind all aspects of human experience (Lazarus, 1991; Damasio, 1995).

Indeed, for a long time, rationality has stood in opposition to the emotional aspect of human nature, and emotions have been considered an irrational force. However, in the 20th century, philosophers such as John Macmurray (1961), neurologists such as Antonio Damasio (1995), and psychologists such as John Heron (1992) and Daniel Goleman (1995) have begun to argue that emotions are deeply associated with human reason, and emotions are central to each individual's perceptions of reality, meaning and personhood.

Macmurray's opening phrase in his book *Reason and Emotion* asserts that 'any enquiry must have a motive or it could not be carried on at all, and all motives belong to our emotional life' (1961, p. 3). He argued that in a conventional sense, the disassociation between reason, as 'a state of mind which is cold, detached and unemotional', and emotions, which belong to another world 'more colourful, more full of warmth and delight, but also more dangerous', is a false dichotomy. This is because reason is more than pure intellect. In the long quote below, Macmurray summarises the main thrust of his argument that emotional reasoning is what makes us human. He wrote:

> Reason—the capacity in us which makes us human—is not in any special sense a capacity of the intellect. It is not our power of thinking, though it expresses itself in our thinking as well as in other ways. It must also express itself in our emotional life, if that is to be human. . . . Reason reveals itself in emotion by its objectivity, by the way it corresponds to and apprehends reality. Reason in the emotional life determines our behaviour in terms of the real values of the world in which we live. . . . The development of human nature in its concrete livingness is, in fact, the development of emotional reason (Macmurray, 1961, p. 49).

Macmurray pointed out that pure intellect which rejects the emotions cannot be a source of action because it also rejects creativity, 'a characteristic which belongs to personality in its wholeness, acting as a whole, and not any of its parts acting separately' (*ibid.*, p. 45). To educate the person in their wholeness is, above all, to allow individuals to develop their sensitivities and emotions. As argued by Macmurray, awareness of the world around us means having a direct 'emotional experience of the real value in the world, and we respond to this by behaving in ways which carry the stamp of reason upon them in their appropriateness and grace of freedom' (*ibid.*).

This view is supported by Damasio (1995) who explained that emotion and rationality are inter-connected and inter-dependent in the brain. Damasio maintains that in classic Western rationality, the emotions are allocated an awkward, inconvenient role in which 'our (rational) hero' is assailed by the emotions portrayed as gods. Emotions are regarded as at odds with thinking and reasoning. Therefore, education and schooling generally stress the intellect at the expense of the emotions.

Macmurray concluded that in contrast to conventional belief, the emotional life is not subordinate or subsidiary to the intellectual life; it is, rather, 'the core and essence of human life' (*ibid.*, p. 75). The intellect and reason find root in the emotions and draw nourishment and sustenance from them. The emotional life is profoundly influential in the flourishing of the whole person because it is in and through the emotional life that human beings develop their unity of personality (both individually and socially). In other words, emotions are the unifying factor in human life.

In the late 20ᵗʰ century, further attempts were made to work in the conceptual space of the 'emotions in learning'. Accordingly, understanding emotions and being able to engage with the feelings and emotions in educational contexts become interesting for writers and commentators. Some authors, such as Daniel Goleman and Howard Gardner, acknowledge that emotions are the 'centre of aptitudes' for human livelihoods, and underpin moral stances and rational thinking (Goleman, 1995; Bar-On & Parker, 2000).

Emotions in narrative encounters

Emotions play an inevitable and essential role in the process of narrative encounter. They are 'a primary feature of our reactions to, or interactions with, narrative' (Pence, 2004, p. 273). It has long been acknowledged that there is a double interpretative process embedded in the narrative encounter—the interpretation of the stories and the interpretation of the act of narration (Ricoeur, 1992). The interpretations can, at the same time, be both analytical and reflective, and motivated by feelings and emotions, and are potentially transformative.

Deslandes (2004, p. 339) supports this view and writes that:

> Acknowledging emotion in its constructive capacity as a means to comprehend the world is to come to terms with emotion's ability to grasp the empirical data of sensible experience.

Deep in the process of narrative encounter and the hermeneutic cycle is our emotional experience which prompts resonance and further emotional experiences. Deslandes (2004) suggests that emotions be necessary components to frame important implications and contribute to decision making. Drawing on Hume's writing, he argues that emotions in the narrative process are characterised by two features: on the one hand, emotions are individual, and on the other, emotions are 'transsubjective entities' that pass on between people (*ibid.*, p. 359).

Often the stories people tell about their lives consist of certain emotional components, which motivate them to pursue a particular path in their onward journeys. These emotional components then become the driving forces for narrated stories. As tellers, we tend to focus on experiences that have triggered some kind of emotional responses from us, and these motivate us to make sense of the events through the narratives. The narrator's interpretation is therefore not limited to a rational and analytical reflection, but an understanding framed by the emotions. In the meantime, the reader/listener finds resonance in the narrator's emotions and is prompted to suggest further interpretations of the narratives.

This means that in narrative encounters, the emotions embedded in the narrator's telling and the emotions that find resonance in the listener are both motivating factors that create opportunities for interpretation, meaning-making and new action.

Encountering each other as whole persons in the narrative process

As pointed out earlier, in the narrative encounter, the collaborators (the teller and the listener) also meet each other on the identity level. This encounter can be a transformative force.

Heinze (2009, p. 275) claims that human personality is not only shaped by affectivity (emotions) but has affectivity as its very condition. In other words, at the core of the person is the emotions, and how people act and react in the world is also emotional in nature, in addition to their moral and ethical responses. Rosfort & Stanghellini (2009, p. 283) maintain that:

> To disregard the affective dimension of human experience and action is a mistake in the sense that we thereby ignore what makes us human, namely, our refined sensibility expressed in the way we are touched by our surroundings.

However, we humans are not just our emotions because we, our narratives and our interpretation of our narratives are always embedded in a given socio-cultural and historical context and in the relationship with those who listen/respond to our stories. This is what Rosfort & Stanghellini (*op cit.*) term the 'fragile dialectic between being (*Sein*) and appearing-to-be (*Schein*)'. Indeed, human personhood is constituted by how we are in the world, how we relate to others and ourselves within given contexts. Furthermore, stories in different cultures depict and inspire emotions in different ways (Hogan, 2003). The way humans react affectively to the world around them might differ from culture to culture and in different social and historical contexts. Therefore our sensitivity to the emotions in the stories and the emotions that drive the stories and our interpretations of the tales can be further crucial junctures for understanding human experience and life history.

Often in an intimate narrative exchange context, both collaborators can develop a deep and emotional understanding of the shared lived experience through bringing in their own voices and languages as well as their emotional selves and biographies. This is also an encounter on the level of identity. The more intention there is to develop a collaborative and narrative relationship, the more the collaborators allow themselves to each become immersed in the emotional world of the other, which might lead to a re-storying experience in a powerful and empathetic way.

Riessman (2005) suggests that 'messy' and 'disorderly' emotions can play an important role in human thoughts about 'the good and the just'. In her reflection on the ethics of her research work conducted in Southern India, Riessman notes that diverse emotions in the research field can serve as sign posts and warnings about what mattered deeply to her, the researcher, and the participants.

We will address the process of establishing, constructing and negotiating such relationships as the basis for narrative collaboration and discovery in the next chapter.

3. The stages of narrative encounter

Having explored the nature of narrative encounter from a hermeneutic perspective, as well as examined emotions and whole-person-ness in engaging in the encounter, we want to move on to revisit the process of life history research and try to extrapolate some insights in terms of the stages of narrative encounter.

The following was proposed as broad stages involved in a life history research encounter (Goodson, 2006):

1. *Narration* —Preparing and sharing narratives of the individual's life as lived. Gill (2007b) suggests that the sharing of stories may include the use of creative methods, such as making drawings, using symbolic objects, writing, poetry, posters, etc., especially when the sharing within a group setting, such as research with a focus group.

2. *Collaboration*—After the initial sharing, the researcher(s) and the participant(s) examine the transcripts and provide and receive feedback from each other. This

is a collaborative process where questions and challenges are posed about meanings in the stories, for the purpose of better understanding the lived experience as told.

3. *Location*—The collaborative reading and understanding of meaning in the narratives is combined with a process of collaborative interpretation and analysis, locating individual stories in their wider historical time and political contexts, social and cultural practices. Often links between individual stories are made to form a picture of a collective experience.

Goodson (2006) suggests that it is important to go through these three stages—narration, collaboration and location, in order to arrive at an account of an individual's full life history, which in itself can allow a holistic understanding of the person and his/her life in context. Gill (2007b) develops the notion of 'location' further when examining the process of teachers' writing their learning biographies (more on this in Chapter Eight) and argues that as the result of analysis and interpretation, critical self-reflection and guided reading and discussion of the relevant literature, these teachers go through two further stages in the process. These two stages are 4) theorisation and 5) direction. Theorisation seemed to allow the teachers to understand from a conceptual point of view what learning is and how learning takes place in an individual's life; direction follows on from the first four stages when the teachers identified themes or topics for their ongoing investigation into their practice as researchers and teachers. The second part of the book will elaborate on these possible stages within the narrative encounter.

Relationships are pivotal to the narrative encounter

The key to the five-stage narrative encounter is the relationship between the narrative collaborators. Self-interpretation is connected to the understanding that is derived from interaction with collaborators or 'interpreters'. Narratives, in this way, are never set apart from a community of interpreters. In narrative and life history research, this could be the relationship between the researcher and her participants. In other narrative encounters, the collaborators are equal partners in the narrative endeavour.

The transformative potential lies in the creation of spaces in which the collaborators can also consider their (shifting) identities and shifting narratives. Conversations and stories are evolving all the time, and each hermeneutic/interpretive cycle brought about by the participants' experience of emotions and motivations will in turn re-structure their told experiences and understanding of the meanings embedded within them. Thus the narrative encounter pivots on relationships where meaning emerges between people in social and historical particularity within dialogic environments (Riessman, 2005).

The dialogic environment is characterised by the reciprocal relationship between the narrator and his/her audience or the narrative collaborators. All narratives (even one's internal conversation) have an intended audience (Koschmann, 1999). The other and the 'alien' are present in all narratives or stories not just in their capacity as the audience or the interlocutor, but also as word which is a two-sided act, its meaning is determined equally by whose word it is and for whom it is meant. As word, it is precisely the product of the reciprocal relationship between speaker and listener, addresser and addressee. (Gadamer, 1977; Voloshinov, 1973).

The reciprocal relationship has been defined by Carl Rogers (1951) as encompassing empathetic understanding, unconditional positive regard, genuineness (realness or congruence), non-directedness and critical thinking. This person-centred approach to interpersonal relationships has been adopted by facilitators of learning in education, counselling and other fields. The goal is to respect others as whole persons who are able to

> take self-initiated action, . . . are capable of intelligent choice and self-direction, . . . are critical learners, . . . have acquired knowledge, . . . adapt flexibly, . . . utilize all pertinent experience freely and creatively, . . . cooperate effectively, . . . [and] work . . . in terms of their own socialized purposes (Rogers, 1951, pp. 387–388).

Rogers (1969) wrote that 'certain attitudinal qualities' embedded in the personal relationship described above can 'yield' significant learning. The first quality would be genuine trust in each other (in a typical life history research context, it is trust in the participant by the researcher; and in a learning context, it is trust in the learner by the facilitator). This is followed by the establishment of an environment or space where there is a feeling of acceptance of each other and empathetic atmosphere. Rogers (1969) maintained that this climate of acceptance is a kind of 'non-possessive caring' and 'operational expression of his essential confidence and trust in the capacity of the human organism' (p. 109), and empathy is 'the attitude of standing in the other's shoes', of viewing the world through the other's eyes (p. 112).

The reciprocal relationship between narrative collaborators does not place one person over the other; rather they mutually facilitate each other's narrative reflections. The qualities discussed above could lead to significant understanding and transformation in a number of ways. For instance, such a relationship might allow fixed narratives—closed and recurring as in the example we gave in Chapter Four, 'I have been . . . therefore I am . . . '—to evolve within the encounter, which is an ongoing process that allows shifts and transformations to 'I have been, and I am and therefore I might be . . .', which is open, retrospective and also prospective.

Challenges and confrontations do not negate the qualities in the reciprocal relationship. On the contrary, without external judgement the narrator is more likely and more able to see the tension and conflicts in his/her own narration and interpretation. The key to achieving a transformative quality in personal narratives is the process of narrative encounter, which in turn, is determined by the dialogic environment and relationship within which the encounter takes place.

4. Reciprocal pedagogy—the interchange of narrative

Although still situated within a life history research context, in this chapter we have gradually brought education and learning endeavour into our discussion about narrative encounter. This is because we believe that the kind of understanding and transformation developed during the narrative encounter is part of human learning. It allows us to move from seeing narrative as research data and then as the research process, to perceiving narrative as sites for pedagogic encounters and learning. Learning, as pointed out earlier, is not the transmission of cognitive abilities and content. Rather it is an interplay of to-and-fro dialogic encounters at the core of which is enhanced understanding of oneself, others, one's place in the world and a course of action more aligned with one's values, beliefs and worldview.

This notion of learning and pedagogy will mean a radical re-examination of relationships in education and in research, in particular, the role of the educator, and the researcher. Plummer (2001) already proposes more radical and liberal political action as the result of narrative and life history research. He maintains that

> researchers should take sides; should study experiences that are biographically meaningful for the researcher; should attend to pivotal turning point experiences; should uncover and display models of truth, accuracy and authenticity; should privilege languages of feelings and emotions over those of rationality and science; should examine multiple discourses and should write multivoiced polyphonic texts, which include the researchers' own experience (p. 13).

Plummer sees this as a 'renewed passionate commitment to a self reflexive, moral and political project in the human and social sciences' (p. 14). This is indeed what Plummer terms 'critical humanism', which he summarises to have five components, that it must

a. pay tribute to human subjectivity and creativity—showing how individuals respond to social constraints and actively assemble social worlds;

b. deal with concrete human experiences—talk, feelings, actions—through their *social and economic organizations* (and not just their inner, psychic or biological structuring);

c. show a naturalistic '*intimate familiarity*' with such experiences—abstractions untempered by close involvement are ruled out. There must be a self-awareness by the sociologist of their ultimate *moral and political role* in moving towards a social structure in which there is less exploitation, oppression and injustice and more creativity, diversity and life;

d. walk a tightrope between a situated ethics of care (recognition, tolerance, respect for persons, love) and a situated ethics of justice (redistribution, equality);

e. espouse an epistemology of radical, pragmatic empiricism which takes seriously the idea that knowing—always limited and partial—should be grounded in experience.

Plummer's critical humanism certainly supports the vision of narrative learning and narrative pedagogy we have tried to propose in this book.

So, to summarise, Gadamer's writing on philosophical hermeneutics points out that narrative encounter is more of a matter of experiencing something new, rather than a mere transmission of cognitive content and 'values'. The encountering something new is not limited to the strangeness in the other but also new and previously unknown aspects in ourselves. The dialogic encounter also stresses the importance of language(s) and the traditions and voices embedded in the language with which we speak, think, and through which we experience our world. Gadamer's notion of 'the dialogue that we are' suggests that dialogic encounter be the essence of narrative pedagogy.

Dewey's writing further supports our suggestion that relationships are key to establishing a trusting dialogic environment. According to Dewey (1916), instead of fear of the alien, dialogic encounter aims to shape a common possession, and in overcoming isolation and creating experiences of emotional closeness and group consensus it achieves the most satisfying of human pleasures (see Waks, 2010). Following Dewey, we would like to propose that encounter allows individuals to form intense friendships, and through that encounter, a community takes shape. It works by means of emotional closeness to generate shared experience and a powerful unity of outlook that breaks down all social barriers. Intense friendships express themselves through dialogic encounter, and encounter in turn reinforces intense friendships. Listening is deep attentiveness; listening is listening with love.

Questions for discussion

In this chapter, we began by examining Gadamer's philosophical hermeneutics and proposed to use this as an interpretive framework to understand the nature of dialogic encounter in the narrative process. By doing so, we highlighted four major components of hermeneutical interpretation that are relevant to our endeavour in the book: the openness to the other, including the otherness of oneself; the importance of attending to the 'alien' or what is new in the narrative during the encounter; an awareness of the interplay of social, cultural and historical traditions which creates the possibilities for new understanding and learning; and finally, the encompassing of the language world that we live in and that confronts us.

We also identified that emotions play a quintessential role in the narrative encounter, and that a close relationship is necessary for attentive listening and forming a community for learning. We concluded that narrating, listening, encountering and friendship serve as the bedrock of narrative pedagogy and learning. It is an important avenue to nurturing individuals who share values with deeper understanding of themselves and others, which form the basis for human flourishing.

Questions that can further our understanding may include the following:

- As narrative collaborators, how do we attend to the otherness in the narrative interchange?
- If an awareness of our own prejudices can be the basis for fusion of horizons, in what way can we employ the questioning in order to develop such awareness?
- How can narrative collaborators make useful sense of the myriad of stories and episodes to develop a third voice?
- If the key to narrative process is reciprocal human relationships, what are the ground rules for developing these relationships? How, for instance, are the issues of differentiated power dealt with? Is there an aspiration to foster egalitarian relationships (albeit on differentiated terrains)?

Suggested Reading

Dewey, J. (1920). *Philosophy of reconstruction.* London: University of London Press.

Gadamer, G. (1977). *Philosophical hermeneutics.* David E. Linge (Ed. and Trans.). Berkeley, CA: University of California Press.

Goleman, D. (2007). *Social intelligence: The new science of human relationships.* New York: Random House.

Grondin, J. (1994). *Introduction to philosophical hermeneutics.* New Haven, CT: Yale University Press.

Myerhoff, B., Kaminsky, M., & Weiss, M. (2007). Stories as equipment for living: *Last talks and tales of Barbara Myerhoff.* Ann Arbor, MI: University of Michigan Press.

Rogers, C. (1961). *On becoming a person. A therapist's view of psychotherapy,* Boston, MA: Houghton Mifflin.

6

Narrative Encounter: Human Agency and Social Action

We shall not cease from exploration
And the end of all our exploring
Will be to arrive where we started
And know the place for the first time.
                    T. S. Eliot, Little Gidding

Introduction

As we discussed in Chapter One, narrative is an inherently human way of con-structing and communicating meaning and expressing human horizons of expe-rience and aspiration. Narrative can be seen as discourse that articulates events, actions and agency within broad social, cultural and historical contexts. Life sto-ries are often the recounting of events and actions that have a temporal element, told in a chronological order and social in character, i.e., all narratives need an audi-ence, even if it is the narrator him/herself in an internal conversation; and final-ly, all life stories have meaning or the narrator's interpretation of meaning. Some may describe this as the moral of the story.

Life narratives, which come in a multitude of forms, shapes and flavours and from diverse sources and origins, are used in many different disciplines and approaches. They can be in the form of auto/biographies, journals, diaries, personal letters, research interviews, photographic journals, TV documentaries, obituaries, CVs, and most recently, personal websites, social networking sites on the internet, blogs, Facebook, Twitter, and video diaries, and other technology-assisted visual story telling media.

In this chapter, we revisit the definition of life narrative and reflect on further questions about the relationship between narrative and selfhood. A starting point is to confront that nagging question—do people seek and present a so-called core self in their narratives? This question will also help us address Pierre Bourdieu's concern for biographical illusion in narrative research. It leads us to examine questions such as: *What forms does life narrative normally take? Does narrative have an embedded structure? How does the way that individuals and groups narrate their lives affect the way they act in the world?* In particular, we will examine the individual and social nature of human narratives in the process and re-emphasise the point made in Chapter Five, that it is the narrative encounter that helps shape the stories that people tell and the actions they take afterwards. Life narratives are therefore not products but processes.

We end this chapter with a case study to briefly illustrate that life history and narrative research have the potential to change each individual's agency and social action within a community and align it with their own values and purpose in life.

1. Narrative and selfhood

There is this nagging question and its derivatives: can life narrative bring out the 'true' self? Is there such thing as a 'core identity' and 'essential self'? Is it possible to have an identity without some kind of life telling? We are fully aware that these questions require the kind of philosophical treatment that this book cannot afford. Nevertheless, we will try to address these questions from our own reading, understanding and experience. Please refer to Chapter One for a more extended review of the various conceptualisations of narrative identity, including the postmodernist views.

The excerpt below provides an unedited version of Charles's first response to our invitation for him to talk about his life. Charles, an adult educator, was 44 at the time of this meeting, is articulate and seems to have some prior idea in terms of what life narrative would mean to a person. He appears to have adopted this strategy in his own telling: setting the scene by introducing his background including his family; recounting his life more or less linearly, i.e., starting with accounts of key moments in childhood, an account of schooling experience and important (and traumatic) incidents, college and university studies, a recollection of his working life in his 20s and 30s and relationships during this time; before moving on to more recent events. In this excerpt, we deliberately left Charles' account as one long paragraph.

Scherto: As we have explained, we are broadly interested in how people understand themselves and live their lives accordingly. So the idea is really for you to tell us about yourself, and you can decide how you wish to tell me and we might later have some questions, and will have a conversation together.

Charles: I think this is about how one makes sense of one's life. In order to make sense of my life, so I think maybe just, I'll mention a couple of those things that put everything else into context. First of all my life's felt incredibly rich and in fact I've lived a few lives in one, in many ways. I suppose that's the same for everybody, but certainly for me and it is something that many people find strange and that people have commented on. It's a common phrase 'you've had so many different lives,' and I'd have to agree, you know, that it's true. The other thing is that the motivation of my whole life has always been about understanding me—who I am, and that's really taken priority above everything else and that's always been through reflection. So the main things in my life that I would talk about, the main incidents that stick with me are incidents where there has been some quite, quite fundamental kind of issue or difference or struggle or something that led to some kind of greater understanding, or some kind of learning, yeah, learning of some kind. So whilst there are lots of incidents that have been beautiful and ugly, the main things for me I feel are important are those times in my life where there has been quite a tremendous struggle of some kind or another. So bearing that in mind. I don't know how useful background is, but I was born in south London, premature by two months. I had a twin brother, identical twin brother, which was great. So growing up, I've always had a companion, always had someone else there. You often read sometimes, especially in the 60s, that you are seen as the same person, but my mum, fortunately, was very adamant that we always were in different classes and dressed differently, so that was one way of overcoming that. I have an older brother, older sister. I had another brother who died when we were two. I have vague recollections and memories of him. What I remember more is the drama and the trauma in the household around that time. He had a congenital heart problem. I guess when you're living in a suburb of south London, yeah it was absolutely fine. There was a tremendous amount of freedom which I think people now don't have so much in London and so a very, very strong imaginative life. Things I remember were like lying on my back in the garden watching gnats sort of hovering. Things like strange sort of dreams and incidents, just a very, very strong sort of powerful, imaginative life as well as practical things. That was very much part of me and my brother actually. We used to sort of, my mother tells us we used to have conversations in our sleep. It sounds bizarre but I remember one incident when both of us were sitting up in bed talking to some kind of presence in the room and this presence was spouting some kind of wisdom I think. I didn't understand, but this was very much like, this was very real to us. I think my childhood, if I'm honest, coining a catch phrase, rather than giving a blow by blow account, up until the age of say 11 was very much about fantasy and imagination. We had opportunities to express all of that fortunately, you know, through art, music and all of that stuff. And then my mother, my mother rather than my father, my father was just a different kettle of fish, but my mother very much encouraged some kinds of creative expression, you know, the opportunity to learn an instrument, always in the garden there was a mass of paint and paper everywhere and just, you know, allowing our creative expression free rein. Lots of adventures. At the end of our road there was this kind of tributary to the Thames, just this small river. It was just a kind of concrete thing with a little bit of water in the bottom. We used to imagine that this would lead to the sea, eventually, so we'd go down there, you know, as kids we really believed that if we followed it we'd get to the sea, you know, the sea is a magical place. So hours spent going on adventures . . . I mean as kids back in those days you could go beyond your own road, go and explore and everyone had bikes for example. That gave a tremendous amount of freedom and possibility and see. That was all great, childhood. School I think was fine. Primary school certainly was not a problem . . .

In this excerpt, without any prompt, Charles suggests that one of the motivations in his life is self-understanding, and he has already perceived his life as a reflexive selfhood project. He identifies his life as being 'a few lives', 'rich' and 'multiple' which becomes better defined in his later telling in which he separates his work life as an educator and therapist, his intellectual life as a postgraduate researcher, his spiritual life as a person who follows Buddhism and engages in spiritual practices, his sexuality, and other relationships in life such as being part of his family, friendship, and so on. Nevertheless, he believed (and so he managed to do in the rest of his telling) that through the narratives he was able to make sense of these interconnected aspects and find a way of sewing a patchwork into a meaningful tapestry, showing some causal effects and linkages, with each piece helping to build up the whole picture of himself as a person.

Using life stories to express who we are has been linked to being an individual exercise of self-creation and may thus collude with the emerging confessional culture of self-obsession. Critiques of this aspect of biographical work tend to suggest that narrated life stories be narcissistic self-accounts through which individuals actively create and recreate themselves. Plummer (2001) points out that the current trend for using personal stories is in danger of turning narratives into some kind of commodity for self-promotion and self-advertisement.

Furthermore, as we have already seen in Chapter One, postmodernist thinking would challenge Charles' pre-active assumption of the possibility of understanding one's life and oneself through such narrative coherence. For instance, in Sermijn, Devlieger, & Loots (2008) interview, the narrator, 18-year-old Charlotte, came up with a fragmented account in the excerpt below. The manner of Charlotte's telling is in total contrast with that of Charles in almost every way.

Charlotte: Yeah, . . . let's see, yeah, that's hard. [laughs] Yeah, I just say, that's tricky, it's so hard to start from nothing, . . . Yeah, maybe I'll just tell what I'm thinking right now. . . . So last year, or was it two years ago in the summer, I wasn't happy with myself. I didn't feel fat, but I didn't feel good about myself and I started to eat less and less, I didn't think I was pretty, but I still ate. But I ate less and less and then I noticed that that made me feel good and that I was so strict and imposed these rules on myself. So I did that for a year and it got worse and worse, eating less, eating nothing. It got worse and worse and then I really started to think that I was fat. I think about something else: actually I was already interested in anorexia earlier. I remember that I used to read books, novels about girls who thought they were fat, and once I gave a presentation about it. Maybe that's the reason, what made me actually get it. I don't know. . . . The psychologist says it's other stuff, that it has to do with my relationship with my parents . . . but I don't believe that. I think that maybe it comes from those books. . . . What would my parents have to do with it? . . . Yeah, I knew it wasn't good, but I didn't want to admit that something was wrong because I felt perfect, still not good, but I felt better and better if I ate less and so and when I went to the hospital I had to go to the psychologist every week for an hour and I really liked that. In the beginning it was so hard there . . . then my eating schedule was adjusted. I had to eat more, that was really hard, all these things I never wanted to eat. Now I don't have problems anymore with it. Now I'm completely better. . . . I don't know if I'm really completely better but I feel completely better, but I don't know if I'm completely better. I feel completely better. This period's kind of in the past. Yeah, it's still . . . if I see other girls eating an apple for lunch, then I think, "Uh oh, they have anorexia." I don't want to talk with anyone about it, especially not with girls, it's kind of being scared that others can do what I couldn't. Now I can just . . . if I went out to eat, "Oh no, then I have to eat something again, oh no, not a school trip because then I have to eat again. Oh no," the whole time with food and now school trips aren't a problem and I can go on vacation again with others. There are still some of those things in my head, there are still some of those things, I want to eat healthy: no fries, I never want to eat that, no cake, that kind of thing and still with other girls I notice what they eat. Watch what I eat. I used to think about it all the time when I came home: "Oh, she ate an apple, maybe she'll get skinnier than me." Now it's not like that anymore, now I think "Stupid girl." I still notice that stuff, for instance yesterday there was a girl at school who only ate an apple for lunch. Yeah, just an apple! So now it's all much easier, life's a lot easier. Yeah, and otherwise . . . I have a lot of hobbies, especially sports, tennis and hockey, I really enjoy that and I want to do it well, just like at school. I'm in my last year and get good grades, I expect a lot from myself. . . . Wait a minute, look, this is a photo of my dog who ran away a while ago. When I was six he showed up and my dad wanted a dog and me and the others, my mom and my sisters liked the idea too (Sermijn et al., 2008, pp. 632–633).

We will leave aside the contrasts between the two narrators: Charles being a mature and well-educated middle-class male therapist who prioritises self-understanding as one of his life's projects; Charlotte being a female in late adolescence, whose search for self-identity is a major project at her age, including her having been treated for anorexia; and how the narrators' biographical profiles and stages in their life course might affect the differences in the manner of their telling themselves. Instead, we turn our attention to analyse their distinct approaches to self-narrating from a textual level.

As a way of analysis, Sermijn et al, write:

> the story fragment that Charlotte told me (just like the rest of her tellings) about herself is neither completely coherent nor completely linearly structured around one plot. On the contrary, Charlotte rather told an amalgam of separate—sometimes contradictory—fragments of memories, feelings, events, and ideas. Although some parts of her story do share some traditional story properties, there are just as many contradictory and discontinuous story elements present as well (p. 634).

The authors claim that the implicit expectation of a coherent life story derives from the dominant western perception of autobiographical accounts, which is situated within a temporarily linear and coherent plot and unity which 'turns the story (and the self) into a linear, structured whole' (*ibid.*). They argue, following Butler and Foucault, that the way individuals narrate their life does not necessarily share the universal story's characteristics and that all stories, even the traditional ones, are 'the effects of discourse, creations that are used within certain subcultures' (*ibid.*). Serimijn et al.'s view further contradicts the ideas that a narrative structure is inherent in human storytelling. See Section 3 of this chapter for more discussion on this.

Indeed Serimijn et al. (2008) continue to highlight a number of characteristics of the postmodern approach to understanding life stories:

> Adopting the postmodern story notion, we could view the self as an untamed story, a story that consists of a heterogeneous collection of horizontal and sometimes "monstrous" story elements that persons tell about themselves and that are not synthesized into one coherent story from which they derive their selfhood. This vision—the narrative self as a postmodern story—is related to the postmodern idea that the self has no stable core but is multiple, multivoiced, discontinuous, and fragmented (p. 636).

In our view, this division between the view that the self is coherent and continuous and that of the postmodernists illustrated in Serimijn et al.'s (2008) article reflects a lack of agreement over the definition of the most fundamental concepts such as identity, self, selfhood. In Chapter One, we offered our view of the notion of identity, in particular, we pointed out that one approach to understanding identity is through self-identification and self-characterisation. We propose that both the views above share the notion that a person tends to have multiple ways of identifying him or herself, and these diverse identifications constitute voices and parallel story elements that do not necessarily converge in the attempt to tell a life. The fact that Charles appears to be well organised in his own narrative portrayal of himself and Charlotte's apparent lack of effort to structure her narrative elements may not be a fundamental contrast between the 'traditional' (as referred to by Serimijn et al.) and the 'postmodern' views. The major difference between these two life accounts lies in Charles' ability to sustain and keep going his particular personal narrative despite his multitude of roles, identifications and community memberships; whereas Charlotte does not seem to take a reflexive approach to do this, resulting in a highly fragmented account that does not seem to have any coherence. It is possible that Charlotte also offered narrative elements about herself in order to meet the needs of the researcher, which supports postmodernist theorisation with regard to the narrative fluidity and shifting identity depending on the discourse contexts and the interlocutors.

In this chapter, we have returned to the question about the notion of identity and selfhood in postmodernity already explored in Chapter One. We have used two examples to draw the contrast between the so-called traditional view of selfhood' as 'coherent', 'unitary', with an essential 'core', and the postmodern conceptualisation of it as being 'fragmented', 'shifting', 'fluid', 'multiple', and 'vague'. These are perhaps not the best examples, but we hope that we have raised the issue clearly. That is, we believe that the question is not about whether there is such a thing as an essential core self or a fragmented shifting self. Rather, it is how social researchers and individuals define selfhood, identity and the dynamic interaction between differing narratives, the individual, and their ways of being in the world. In other words, the core elements in the selfhood project are so contested that the focus of the debate is more about the significance of it for human life, instead of about agreeing on the meaning of basic concepts.

2. Is life narrative 'biographic illusion'?

Embedded in the notion of narrative selfhood is the misconception that all life stories are mere personal testimonies of selves and persona. Can human beings' existential reflections free them from the historical, social and cultural constraints and the perspectives developed and embedded in them? Plummer (2001) suggests that one person's tale can be the story of a whole people. Are all our stories merely our individual creation or are they also imposed on us? In other words, are narratives forms of socialisation and enculturation? Where does the scripted narrative come from, such as: I am a working class, black, single mother and I live the life of a black working class single mother? Are most people associated with and do they subscribe to the kind of image and perception of themselves as persons who are the products of culture and social power dynamics?

Memories, argues Plummer, are not simply psychological attributes; they are social events, which individuals and groups attach themselves to. They are tales of how things were, why things were, and how things are and might be. He writes:

> Thus any genealogy of an auto/biographical society must now start to detect the moments when various tales of the outcast, the marginal and the silenced begin to appear and how they come to take a hold in the imagination of a wider society (2001, p. 91).

Plummer considers those outcast's tales as bringing with them spaces for more voices to enter the social research world, including voices of Holocaust survivors, lesbians and gays, stories about aging, health, and HIV/AIDS, and tales about indigenous peoples who have been colonised. Plummer further uses women's auto/biographies and Personal Narratives Groups' work as an example to suggest that they bring with them 'a different voice and distinctive form: that they are more likely to be understated; have less concern with their own public; and have more 'embeddedness' and connectedness to others' (*ibid.*). In this way, women's personal tales become a way to air private worries in public and social concerns of gender, class, ethnicity, age, health, disabilities, motherhood and other feminist issues.

Highlighting the dynamic relationship between the personal, the social and the historical is a major strength of life history work, as we have seen in the earlier chapters. However, the nature of the research and the authority that the researchers assume in (re)presenting individuals' life stories has been challenged by many. Bourdieu (1994) believes that life history research tends to impose logic and order on otherwise chaotic lives as lived, forcing false coherence and continuity. He terms this 'biographic illusion'. For Bourdieu, the way life history researchers construct individual life narratives and biographies does not necessarily allow for contingencies such as confusion, ambiguity, contradiction, reversion, incoherence and the irrelevance of events. Bourdieu argues that life as the fulfilment of the individual's personal project, through the succession and order of events shaped into the person's characteristics and the unity of identity, is an illusion.

Indeed, in life history research, if the researcher has a pre-determined 'map' of the landscape in mind and surveys the participants' lives in order to 'direct' and 'steer' their life stories towards some kind of pre-assumed coherence, then the illusion-reproach is a useful warning. Meanwhile, if life history work is simply indulging the individual's self-(re)creation, then it underestimates the power of encounter discussed in the previous chapter.

The fact that life narrative is simultaneously individual and social has long been recognised in life history and narrative research. Hence, most researchers have now gone beyond the traditional detached and distanced approach to participants' life stories, where voices are edited out of the researchers' report. Fewer and fewer researchers will present life narratives as a coherent story of the truth about the other as if they themselves are outside the situation being described by a hidden—an unobtrusive camera—reporting, even on their own activities (Denzin, 1997). Instead, the researcher becomes 'a part of the writing project' (*ibid.*), and the research becomes a process of encounter, as described in Chapter Five.

Bakhtin (1984) holds that any narrative, even when it is not placed within a research context, can be 'a conversation of the most intense kind, for each present, uttered, word responds and reacts with its every fibre to the invisible speaker, points to something outside itself, beyond its own limits' (p. 197). This is an important aspect of narrative that we have been trying to emphasise throughout the book. That is, narrative is not a product nor is it a set of tales about individuals and their communities. It is a process, a journey that leads to learning, agency and better understanding of oneself, others and one's purpose in the world. This is not to assume that anyone who tells his/her life will arrive at an ideal destination, where actions and values converge and the onward journey unfolds with the promise of wellbeing and happiness, as in Ricoeur's proposal.

Life stories are not end products but the beginning of the social process of narrative encounter as described in Chapter Five. The five stages we proposed earlier, *narration, collaboration, location, theorisation/meaning-making and direction* (in Chapter Seven, we consolidate and renamed the final stage 'integrity' which is more suitable for our analysis of moral concerns than 'direction' implies), bring together the horizons of the interlocutors or narrative collaborators including their respective life experiences, personal values, and theories (personal and scientific) and concepts. Bourdieu's concern for order and coherence being imposed can thus be ameliorated.

This social process has built into it the unfolding of reciprocal meaning and, to a certain extent, a pursuit of order within a larger whole—social, cultural and personal. In this way, life history and narrative research projects are sites for telling and retelling life stories, for construing and interpreting meaning, and for constructing and reconstructing andividual life's trajectories and communities' collective actions.

3. A closer look at life stories and narrative structure

Often, the structure of narrative consists in the content of a story and the form the narrative uses in order to make sense of a story. These may be described as the story and the plot. From a literary point of view, some authors, such as Christopher Booker (2004), argue that individual life stories bear an overall resemblance to the plots of stories found in literature. Booker maintains that 'wherever men and women have told stories, all over the world, the stories emerging from their imaginations have tended to take shape in remarkably similar ways (*ibid.*, 2004, p. 3). Booker summarises these different stories into what he calls seven basic plots which are: comedy, tragedy, rags-to-riches, the quest, overcoming the monster, voyage and return and rebirth. Booker further holds:

> the more familiar we become with the nature of these shaping forms and forces lying beneath the surface of stories, pushing them into patterns and directions which are beyond the story teller's conscious control, the more we find that we are entering a realm to which recognition of the plots themselves proves only to have been the gateway. We are in fact uncovering nothing less than a kind of hidden, universal language: a nucleus of situations and figures which are the very stuff from which stories are made. And once we become acquainted with this symbolic language, and begin to catch something of its extraordinary significance, there is literally no story in the world which cannot then be seen in a new light: because we have come to the heart of what stories are about and why we tell them (p. 6).

We believe that there are also cultural archetypes in the shape and form of individual stories, which create archetypes of persona and power structures that affect people's experience of events and individual and group agency. It is therefore very important to understand that we cannot use 'story' as a monolithic term because there are so many varieties. Story can be culturally inscribed. For example, some cultures may inscribe a grandiose self where individuals celebrate their own glorified images, whereas other cultures may approach the individual's sense of identity from a degree of theoretical detachment.

Other authors argue that human psyches have also influenced the way life narratives are constructed. McAdams's (1993) psychology of identity broadly agrees with Booker in that he recognises archetypes (tragedies, comedies, romance and irony) in the life stories individuals construct, but ultimately, he argues that humans are storytellers, and it is through telling that they develop self-knowledge and meaning with a sense of coherence. This is achieved by creating personal myths. He writes:

> This is not the stuff of delusion or self-deception. We are not telling ourselves lies. Rather, through our personal myths, each of us discovers what is true and what is meaningful in life. In order to live well, with unity and purpose, we compose

a heroic narrative of the self that illustrates essential truths about ourselves. Enduring human truths still reside primarily in myth, as they have done for centuries (1993, p. 11).

From a psychological perspective, McAdams suggests that a personal myth is 'an act of imagination that is the patterned integration of our remembered past, perceived present and anticipated future' (*ibid.*, p. 12). Whether it is the myth of gods and goddesses, or heroes and heroines, such as warriors, sages, lovers, caregivers, healers and survivors, personal myths are not pre-formed characters waiting to be recognised. Rather, McAdams proposes, humans create themselves through myth. Myth-making is a lifelong endeavour and includes childhood's innocent role play, adolescents' trying out different characters, adulthood's internalising characters and resolving tensions, and seeking to 'bring opposing parts of our story together into a vitalising and harmonious whole' (*ibid.* p. 14). McAdams' thesis is that we all identify, live and change our myths through narrative and thus find integrity in life.

However, although stories may have embedded within them archetypes (of events), myths, personas and life courses, life and stories are not the same, even though authors such as Booker, McAdams and others would support the idea that humans act out their stories in 'real' life. Returning to our earlier point (see Chapter One), the relationship between life and narrative is a complex one. On the one hand, life is lived and is often chaotic and lacks the temporal structure that fictional stories have. At the same time, stories are told and are made coherent by the narrator through the selection of events and the structuring of the narrative. This is a highly culturally contingent process and we must be constant in our scrutiny of the danger that Western visions of the selfhood may colonise our discussion and discourse. Therefore, there is always a difference between life as 'lived' and life as 'told'. On the other hand, human actions are always found within the bounds of individual life narratives, biographies, and the stories told to themselves and to others. As Ricoeur (1984) suggests, time and history become human when narrative is a condition of temporal existence. That is to say, narrative has the power to reconfigure the human imagination of past, present and future actions. Therefore, life can be understood and acted upon through the narrative people tell about themselves and their communities.

At the heart of the narrative is the plot. Ricoeur defines plot as 'an integrating dynamism that draws a unified and complete story from a variety of incidents, in other words, that transforms this variety into a unified and complete story' (1992, p. 8). Using this definition, Ricoeur was able to derive the function of the 'integrating components of social change' in the plot. Any order expressed in the narratives is within the realm of the productive imagination of the narrator, which is constituted by the particular cultural schemata and tradition he/she is part of. Thus Ricoeur suggests that '(e)ach of these three points allows us to see in emplotment the correlate of a genuine narrative understanding that precedes, both in fact and by right, every construction of narrating in terms of a second-order rationality' (p. 19).

Ricoeur explores the structure of life narrative through his thesis on mimesis and narrative identity. Mimesis is imitation of nature (in Aristotle and Plato's definition) and imitation of an action. It is not to mimic the action but rather to configure it by imposing an organisation and order of events into a whole. Mimesis is narrative emplotment. Ricoeur distinguishes between the lived experience or the world of action and the imagined world or fiction, which is found in the three senses of mimesis.

Mimesis 1 is the prefiguration of human action. According to Ricoeur,

> To imitate or represent action is first to preunderstand what human acting is, in its semantics, its symbolic system, its temporality. Upon this preunderstanding, common to both poets and their readers, emplotment is constructed and, with it, textual and literary mimetics. (1984, p. 64)

This suggests that the emplotment of narrative cannot be detached from the 'real' world of experience and action within its culture—norms, practices, rules and symbols. Furthermore, actions are characterised by a temporal structure which can only be unfolded through narrative.

Mimesis 2 is the configuration of experience and the organisation of events. It is the representation of action in text, and is the 'postunderstanding of the order of action and its temporal features' (Ricoeur, 1984, p. 65). Through this configuration and representation of time, the narrative integrates the historical (what happened in the past) with the fictional (what could happen in the future) and together it invites the reader's engagement by affecting his or her imagination. This allows the art of narrative to not only unify successions of events over time but also to create the stories of the narrator's community.

Lastly, mimesis 3 is the refiguration which is a response from the reader/listener to the text or the narrative, and/or what the reader/listener brings to mimesis 1 and 2. In other words, the narrative process can only become complete when the reader/listener refigures the plot and thus reinterprets the meaning of the narrative. Ricoeur claims that a text, or narrative, can act on the reader/listener and affect that person in profound and sometimes transformative ways. On this point, Ricoeur concurs with Gadamer in his approach to understanding through the 'fusion of horizons' in that the narrator's perspectives and his/her cultural context and symbolism can be brought together with those of the reader/listener, resulting in new interpretations of human action within the context of history and culture. Within the temporal nature of human action, narratives link the past to the present and place the present in the context of the aims for the future.

Ricoeur's thesis suggests that there is no better way of understanding oneself and one's actions and grasping one's life events from the perspectives of a meaningful whole other than through the creative power of narratives. Life stories and their inherent narrative structure as Ricoeur proposes above also bring forth the values and beliefs that are embedded in each community which frames the narrator's motives, intentions and goals in life. As discussed in Chapters One and Two, narratives enable all of us potentially to understand human actions from an ethical dimension, and every story can teach us something about ways of being with others and within a wider community. This is an essentially Aristotelian view of ethics which postulates that the virtuous life is the good life of human flourishing and fulfilment. Narrative is an ongoing search for the meaning and alignment of actions with intentions and goals. Ricoeur further proposes that narrative ethics have to be rooted in a just society, an ultimate 'raison d'être' of social institutions and communities.

In summary, a closer look at the nature of life stories and Booker, McAdams and Ricoeur's conceptions of the narrative structure embedded in the telling of stories takes the discussion to the realm of narrative ethics, human wellbeing and happiness. However, despite the emplotment of human life stories and human interpretative capability to impose order and meaning on successions of life events and actions, it is not yet clear if all narrators can aspire to such transformative understanding of themselves, others and ways of being within the wider communities. It is to the latter question that we turn next. In particular, we will examine how both the individual and social nature of life narratives and the dialogic encounter help people shape their stories; and finally, how life stories become reflexive and how and when reflexivity leads to renewed human action.

4. The impact of narrative encounter

The exploration of narrative encounter in Chapter Five, and further investigation into the structure of narratives and their inherent personal and social dynamics in this chapter, allow us to point out that life history and other biographical work provide a dialogic space for deeper encounters. Through this process, personal narratives are created and constructed to bring together socially and culturally embedded and constantly shifting discourses and a multitude of self-identifications. Such encounters go beyond 'unfolding' one's subjective experience of life events. They have the potential for changing one's course of action and aligning it with one's own values and purpose in life. This certainly applies to all the narrative collaborators in the dialogic exchange—the researcher(s) and the participant(s). We see the narrative encounter as a kind of unintentional 'intervention' and will illustrate this by offering an example of how narrative shifts as the result of interview conversations.

George is a fifty-year-old black male. He grew up in Belize in Central America, then moved to Honduras, and later migrated to Canada where the interviews began. These interview conversations took place over a year. In total, twelve such interviews were undertaken and each lasted around three hours. The interviews moved from an initial narration with few probing questions or interruptions through to highly collaborative 'grounded conversations' where the life history research interrupted George's own flow of an 'internal conversation' and where he began to reflect and locate his stories within a 'culturally provided script' as he called it, and to re-elaborate and understand his narrative in new ways. The following excerpt was the first part of George's transcript, which was edited slightly.

At school, teachers loved me. When I look back now this was inevitable, I got along with them quite well. In Grade Four you have a crush on your teacher, and I distinctly recall having a crush on this teacher, Miss Janet Jones. She liked me very much. My big thrill was that I would go to her house on Saturdays and wash her bicycle. Bicycles, then, were the way of getting around, and as a result, people took exceedingly good care of them. They would polish them and clean every spoke. After I had washed her bicycle, I could ride it. So there I was, quite proudly tooling around the city riding Miss Jones's bicycle. In a different environment it would be the equivalent of a teacher lending a car. We didn't have bicycles ourselves, so I would visit my classmates and friends they knew I was riding teacher's bicycle.

Education officers visited our school, and they appeared to us as powerful figures. They went beyond the white shirt and tie to suit jackets. Very nice. To us, these guys were the pinnacle of professional achievement. We looked up to them.

After that, it was on to St. Paul's College. That was also a very good experience as I continued to be quite enthusiastic and hard working. St. Paul's College had speech night at the end of every school year. There was a prize for every subject area. Of course, being the academic, highly competitive person I was, I always tried to get a couple of prizes, and always did, at least win something. I never forget how proud I always made my mother, God rest her soul. It was her son, and this is St. Paul's College. I mean, after all we are talking about a place that had no university. Years after I graduated from high school, there was still no university, which is why I didn't go to university until I left the country. Of course, some people did stick their noses to the grindstone and go to University from there, but I didn't. Speech night was very important because in a class of twenty or thirty boys, two or three would be getting all the prizes. It wasn't that spread out because it was mainly an Arts School: History, Geography, Language, Health Science, Mathematics—but Algebra and Physical Geometry, not Trigonometry, no Science. Our school didn't have a science programme at all. Later on, when the government opened a technical school in the north part of the city, some of us were encouraged, because they thought we could do it, half way along, to drop a couple of subjects from our regular curriculum. So, for example, I dropped Health Science and Geography and in the evenings I went over to this school and took Chemistry and Physics. But, anyway, that programme didn't work out well because we were well along in our exercises when we had to take the GCE. At that time it was called the Cambridge School Certificate. High school was very enjoyable. A person who has been a prominent person in my life is my high school English teacher, Howard Robinson. He has since gone on to be one of the outstanding intellectuals in the country. He received his B.A. in English from U.C.W., and his Ph.D., with a thesis on the Creole language as spoken in Belize, in England. He was my mentor throughout my high school years.

After I finished high school I got into teaching. At that time you could enter teaching in two different ways. You could stay on after elementary school and become a teacher's aide, then by taking exams, obtain your first class teacher's certificate. This would take about five years. Alternatively, you could teach once you completed high school. I graduated high school in November and started teaching in January. It makes sense, as far as content is concerned. You certainly learn enough in high school to teach elementary school. In university Ph.D.s teach M.A. There's not that much difference. Once I started teaching, I did in-service-training, with courses in methodology, psychology, and classroom methods and management. I travelled to the district capital once or twice a week to attend classes. After two years I received my first class teacher's certificate. About that time a teacher's college opened, but most who went there didn't have high school [education]. I think there was certain elitist attitude there about high school. I taught elementary for three years from the time I was eighteen'. . . .

I taught elementary for three years in two rural schools. In the second I was the vice-principal. An older woman was the principal and I think the powers wanted me to stay on and eventually take over the school. But I don't think it was meant to be; I didn't see that as what I really wanted to do. I didn't know what I wanted to do, but I think that way back in my head was always the notion that I would leave Belize, and that I would never want to stay there. It always struck me that it was a place that would eventually end up being quite stifling. That may not be so. I know a lot of my ex-classmates who ended up getting a university education and are quite well placed and they seem to love it. But I think I'm the kind of person who prefers to swim in a larger pond. Even though I might be anonymous in that pond, [it is better] than to rule in a very, very, small little puddle and to move in a sort of almost claustrophobic world. That had never appealed to me.

Education is very important in Belize. There is one radio station, Radio Belize. Since there was no university there, anyone leaving the country to study was a news item. The radio would announce: departing from Belize Airport today is A, son of B and C of 1 D street, he is making his way to E to study R. Then four years later, when he returned the event was announced. Conquering Hero. This was a very important thing, because in a country where high school education couldn't be taken for granted, a person with a degree was a deity, really! You could get a degree in anything and be considered super smart. So when a person returned to Belize International Airport, even Cambridge School Certificates were announced on the radio. Students from all over the country got together in Belize City to take the exam in this huge hall, with proctors walking up and down. The exams were then sent to England to be graded and marked. Several months later the results were announced on Radio Belize, they would state the school and the class of the certificate. This radio station was the only one in the whole country, education is a very powerful thing to Belizians; they give education very high value. You want to be one of those announced on the radio for passing your school certificate, and, maybe, one day announced as departing the International Airport. I'm just making this connection right now, this powerful thing, imagining the poor guys who didn't make it through high school. You know there is a certain class there, there's a definite thing, you either have a high school education or you don't! You either have a university education or you do not. It's like that. It's funny though, much as they had a university education, obviously something I dreamed of in a way, my not having a university education made it seem too out of reach for me. Because if you wanted to go to university, there were two ways of doing it, you could win a government scholarship or you could have your parents pay for you. Our family couldn't afford it; in fact if I had not won a scholarship to high school I wouldn't have had a high school education.

One of the fascinations of the dialogic collaboration is to see how intensive 'grounded conversations' and introspective reflection combine to allow the life storytellers to 'locate' their storied experience within broader social, cultural and historical context. George spoke of this process towards the end of the interview:

Looking back, I feel I betrayed the academic promise I showed as a child. Examining the tapes and transcripts had dislodged a number of memories and subsequent feelings. On Monday, I felt quite depressed. I realise that life had passed by. I was troubled by thoughts of what should have been. At this stage I should be a professor or an executive with a house and car. Where have twenty-five years gone?

A university degree is very important to me; I always envied those who returned to Belize with one. I appreciate there are complex reasons behind this. Part of me doubts my ability to do university studies. I don't know if I've got what it takes. However, at some point I made choices. I avoided putting my abilities to the test. Although I didn't articulate it at the time, on reflection—I escaped. I chose a different path. I was a womaniser who ignored my intellectual potential. Eventually I chose marriage over studies. Within my own family, my stepfather, a driver, was an incorrigible womaniser. In high school, despite my academic success I was rebellious and made trouble for the teacher, largely through my quick wit. I avoided further education, but felt frustrated. I now perceive leaving St. Paul's for Honduras as running away because I didn't want to be trapped. I knew I wanted a university degree but wasn't prepared to face the challenge so I quit. I didn't want to be edged out; I didn't want to be an anachronism.

Honduras seemed the logical choice since I was born there. I now see this journey as a flight from self, or from destiny. Only by attending university could I be announced: arriving at the airport . . . I don't really know whether I wanted that, *living out a culturally provided script.*

The main feature of George's narrative elaboration is the way in which he is able to transcend his original national and social background through physical and mental movement and imagination. Here both George and Ivor, his interviewer, experienced considerable contextual instability in the original interaction and later, particularly through their experiences as migrants. (Ivor moved from England to Canada and George from Central America to Canada.) It is almost as if George's narration and narrative learning and understanding held them together during the perilous journey.

Furthermore, George's location of his narrative as 'living out a culturally provided script' marks a clean watershed moment in his understanding of his life. In fact, this narrative encounter coincided with Ivor and George's own transitions—Ivor at the end of this project returned to England to work and George went off to teach in Northern Canada.

In some ways, the construction of a personally elaborated narrative is itself a site of action and learning. Goodson (2010, forthcoming) has argued that narrative construction can be seen as 'primal learning'—learning developed within the central heartland of selfhood. Primal learning is deeply engaged self-development.

In this sense, primal learning foregoes the link between learning and ongoing self understanding and identity construction. Perhaps the most efficacious kind of learning is that which leads to significant shifts in our sense of selfhood.

Above all, we argue that primal learning is informally linked to personal visions of selfhood through the act of ongoing narration. Most people have a root narrative that they relate their life to, but not all people continuously narrate and re-narrate their lives. Primal learning and narrative are therefore intimately linked, so much so that it may be best to refer to this kind of learning as narrative learning.

Narrative learning actually has two favoured 'sites'. Firstly, employing our central root narrative as a tool for learning; secondly and perhaps more crucially, the on-going act of narration and re-narration—the modification and adaptation as well as the verbal reiteration of our life narrative. Narrative encounter becomes the site for the fluid and flexible narrative response to new circumstances and opportunities—it is the dialogic encounter that provides the opportunity to maximise our learning readiness, agency possibilities and ongoing identity construction.

The narrative project thus conceived also has the potential for transforming individuals' perceptions, self-understanding and their courses of action. It can also change a group's collective action, and by transforming the memories and understanding of past experiences, it may help change the way groups or communities interact and prosper together. We will elaborate on this in Chapter Seven and Chapter Eight.

Questions for discussion

This chapter sets up a series of questions for discussion about the nature and purpose of narratives. In light of the dilemma of postmodernist conception of identity and selfhood, we confronted it further by looking at two excerpts of personal narrative intended to communicate about who the person is. Following Booker, McAdams and Ricoeur's theses on narrative structure, we established that adopting a certain personal myth or emplotment can enable individuals to re-examine their stories and relive their narrative in ways that unite their identity, commitment and action. A further excerpt offered an opportunity to witness how this is happening through a dialogic encounter.

It concludes that life history and other biographical work is itself an act of meaning-making through a profound narrative encounter. Life stories, (auto)biographies, personal and communal histories, myths, and other literary genres of self-meditation are ultimately tales about human experiences, actions and ways of being in the world. Narrative is not a product or the object of analysis and interpretation; rather it is a process of dialogic and reciprocal encounter and learning and it is an essential expression of being human. We would like to think that life history and biographical work honour the humanity within each of us as it is engaged in a process of encounter and openness through relationship and true listening.

Questions remain:

- Do life narratives present an 'essential core self' in their accounts? Why or why not? In what way?
- Do you notice in your own field experience any life narratives that follow a series of dominant 'archetypes' found in the wider society in historical contexts?
- How can one justify narration as one of the most 'productive' routes to a) wider understandings, b) self-construction?
- If what we are after is a renewed narrative and changed course of action, in what way does life narrative differ from therapy?

Further reading

Bakhtin, M. (1981). *The dialogic imagination.* Austin, TX: University of Texas Press.

Barthes, R. (1975). An introduction to the structural analysis of narrative. *New Literary History, 6,* 237–262.

Czarniawska, B. (2004). *Narrative in social science research.* Thousand Oaks, CA: Sage.

Deleuze, G. (1990). *The logic of sense.* New York: Columbia University Press.

Holstein, J., & Buberium, J. (2000). *The self we live by: Narrative identity in a postmodern world.* New York & Oxford: Oxford University Press.

McAdams, D., Josselson, R., & Liebich, A. (2006). *Identity and story, creating self in narrative.* San Francisco: American Psychological Association.

Pagnucci, G. (2004). *Living the narrative life: Stories as a tool for meaning making.* Portsmouth, NH: Boynton/Cook.

7

Learning and
Narrative Pedagogy

Man differs from the lower animals because he preserves his past experiences. . . . man lives in a world where each occurrence is charged with echoes and reminiscences of what has gone before, where each event is a reminder of other things. . . . man remembers, preserving and recording his experiences.

We naturally remember what interests us and because it interests us. The past is recalled not because of itself but because of what it adds to the present. Thus the primary life of memory is emotional rather than intellectual and practical. . . . To revive it and revel in it is to enhance the present moment with a new meaning, a meaning different from that which actually belongs either to it or to the past. . . . the conscious and truly human experience . . . comes when it is talked over and re-enacted . . . into a whole of meaning . . .

John Dewey, *Reconstruction in Philosophy,* 1920, pp. 1–3

Introduction

In this book, our major task is to explore how life narratives can be pedagogic sites and to work towards the theory of narrative pedagogy. To do so, we started by defining what narrative is and the part it plays in social research in general and the challenges that this approach confronts (Chapters One and Two). We also examined the process of life history research, individuals' narrative characters and possible shifts in an individual's narratives as the result of dialogic interaction and reciprocal encounters and exchanges (Chapters Three & Four). Then we investigated more closely the nature of the narrative encounter and began to move away from life history research as the site for narrative exchange to a focus on exploring narrative as a pedagogic site and process for learning and transformation (Chapter Five). By doing so, we also looked at how narratives connect with an individual's identity and agency (Chapter Six).

In this chapter, we further expand on the concept of narrative learning and begin to develop a theoretical framework for narrative pedagogy. We also look at how educators can take opportunities offered by encounters to facilitate profound learning.

1. The potential of narrative learning for consolidation and transformation

So far, we have established that as a fundamental form of meaning-making, narratives can be significant sites for individual learning. In this way, a person's sense of self is embedded in the narrative construction. To be a person is not only to be connected to the narrative, but more importantly, it is to be connected to how a person lives his life in relation to that narrative.

Implicit in this argument is a definition of learning which goes beyond the conventional perception of learning as the acquisition of knowledge and skills. Our vision for learning encompasses meaning-making, connecting to what is valuable and worthwhile in what humans do, being and becoming. Indeed, this vision can be so difficult to pin down that many theorists tend to define it under the broad theme of identity development. Thus for some, the narrative project becomes an identity project.

We, however, would rather approach this from a slightly different angle and stress our conception of learning which is centred round the notion of human development. We don't want to call it an identity project per se. For us, learning concerns the flourishing of individual human beings and the realisation of their fullest capacities. Thomson (1987, 2002) argues that the nature of human life must be taken into consideration in order to define 'flourishing' and that a flourishing life must involve appreciating activities that are non-instrumentally valuable (i.e., not a means to an end). Gill & Thomson (2009) further maintain that learning involves the cultivation or strengthening of the personal qualities that are necessary for a flourishing life. These qualities or virtues are more than traditionally conceived knowledge or skills because they involve caring in appropriate ways. They are qualities or virtues that a person should foster independently. These qualities are also to be defined by the general contours of flourishing and by its specific human content appropriate to each person. These qualities are not those required by the 'shoulds' of social morality but rather by the 'it would better if' of personal ethics.

Learning as cultivating of virtues and qualities, can be complicated to define, nevertheless we will attempt here to explore this further. Following Aristotle, Gill & Thomson (2009) argue that for each area of life, there is a corresponding set of virtues or qualities of character (also see Nussbaum, 1988). These qualities stress, amongst other things, being able to appreciate and care for others, (caring for others also requires that one cares for oneself); having inner strength, emotional ability and openness; being able to understand, including having an appropriate appreciation of the relevant aspects and facets of the world; having good judgment, which involves knowing when and how to be critical, and when and how to be open or creative in the sense of looking for new ideas and connections; being open to the views of others and being able to reformulate or reframe problems; being proactive and having something worth caring about, including self-motivation and the ability to take initiatives, work with others; having determination as well as carefulness; having a direction in life suited to one's own nature and talents; respecting and caring for oneself; having a rich inner life.

Perceiving learning from the angle of qualities or virtues helps learning to be conceptualised as the development of the mind, body, heart, and spirit—it is about being and becoming. The notion of learning as human development or human becoming involves understanding oneself appropriately, shifts in each individual's ways of being in the world that are more suited to his/her nature and dispositions, embedding in a web of relationships with the self and others (Arendt, 1958) as well as acting in accordance with each person's specific missions in the world.

In this way, we are beginning to see that learning through narrative encounter has transformative potential. Indeed, scholars could challenge us by saying: look, transformative theorists have been exploring the narrative dimensions of transformative learning. So is narrative learning merely new jargon? Or does it work differently from what is being theorised as transformative learning? If so, then how?

In order to respond to these questions, a brief review of transformative learning theories is useful before exploring how life narratives can facilitate learning that is transformational, but does not necessarily fall within the confines of transformative learning theory. There is no space here to compare the similarities and differences between narrative learning and transformative learning, and we will leave the discussion of their respective conceptual premises for another opportunity. However, we feel it necessary to place narrative learning and transformative learning next to each other, even if only briefly, in order to construct a theory of narrative pedagogy that aims to facilitate the learner's holistic growth as a human being.

Transformative learning theory was first conceived and developed by Jack Mezirow (1978) through a study of women returning to education after an extended hiatus. Mezirow's study suggested maturity progresses from childhood to adulthood where ideals, values and beliefs are first assimilated and constructed through upbringing, schooling and other socio-cultural influences, then reshaped and even transformed in adulthood through education and learning. Transformation, according to Mezirow, involves alienation from earlier established conceptions of values and one's actions in the world, 'reframing new perspectives, and re-engaging life with a greater degree of self-determination' (Mezirow, 2000: xii). Mezirow characterises the process as 'a praxis, a dialectic in which understanding and action interact to produce an altered state of being' (*ibid.*).

Critical self-reflection on a cognitive level was perceived as the key to adult transformative learning theory. So is meaning-making. In transformative learning theory, learning is 'understood as a continuous effort to negotiate contested meanings' (Mezirow 2000:3). He maintains that adult transformative learning is a process of making sense and interpreting the individual's experience through heightened awareness and understanding, re-examining assumptions, synthesising and justifying. By so doing, the person is able to act upon the new meaning perspectives.

In an earlier book, Mezirow (1991, p. 161) holds that transformative learning focuses on perspective transformation, and it involves (a) an empowered sense of self, (b) more critical understanding of how social relationships and culture have shaped his/her beliefs and feelings, and (c) more functional strategies and resources for taking action.

Transformative learning involves experiencing a deep, structural shift in thought, feelings, and actions. It is a shift of consciousness that dramatically and permanently alters each person's way of being in the world. Mezirow identifies ten phases in perspective transformation (1978, 1995):

- A disorienting dilemma
- Self-examination with feelings of guilt or shame
- A critical assessment of assumptions
- Recognition that one's discontent and process of transformation are shared and that others have negotiated a similar change

- Exploration of options for new roles, relationships, and actions
- Planning a course of action
- Acquisition of knowledge and skills for implementing one's plans
- Provisionally trying out new roles
- Building of competence and self-confidence in new roles and relationships
- A reintegration into one's life on the basis of conditions dictated by one's new perspective (summarised in E. Taylor, 1998, p. 4).

Over the last three decades, critiques and further developments in transformative learning theory have created space for educators and researchers to reflect and discuss adult learning in more profound ways.

The first and foremost challenge to Mezirow's model concerns critical reflection. According to Mezirow, critical reflection is a process by which we all attempt to justify our beliefs, either by rationally examining assumptions, often in response to intuitively becoming aware that something is wrong with the result of our thoughts, or challenging their validity through discourse with others of differing viewpoints and arriving at the best informed judgment (Mezirow, 1995, p. 46). Critical reflection described in transformative learning theory is heavily embedded in human rationality. We believe that learning perceived in this way risks underestimating the significance of relationships, discursive and dialogic encounters, emotional and spiritual experience, and even the unconsciousness as part of the holistic endeavour that we have so strongly promoted in this book. Recent developments in transformative learning have included the symbolic, the narrative, the mythological, or the soul dimensions (Dirkx, 1997), as well as using (auto)biographies and other personal narratives as learning tools.

Central to the pedagogy for transformative learning is the way in which educators create opportunities for adult learners to experience disorientation dilemmas, a prerequisite for Mezirow's transformative learning, for instance, feelings of ambiguity, uncertainty and paradox. It is in this respect that narrative learning takes a different path to transformative learning. Narrative learning does not rely on an experience of disorientation in order to question the premises of one's values or beliefs, nor is it necessary for a person to feel critical and discontented about his/her own assumptions. Transformation through narrative learning is enhanced understanding about oneself and the other, one's lived experience as a person over time, one's position in the world, and how histories, cultures and socio-political forces have helped shape who we, as human beings were, who we are now, and the journey we have travelled so far and the journey we are to travel together.

Life does not always contain disorientation dilemma and transitions. Much of life is lived in a routinised even mundane key. Whilst narrative learning and pedagogy can sometimes transform, in many other ways it is about consolidating who we are or delineating courses of action to reflect our own nature. In other words, narrative learning as a lifelong process has an open agenda, and narrative learning draws heavily from one's life and lived experience as well as depends on the individual's narrative characters, the nature of his/her life's vision and life course stage and age. It is not problem-focused and does not intend to resolve dissonances, although narrative pedagogues might find themselves wanting to draw the individual's attention to the discords and dissonances in his/her accounts as pedagogical leverages. We will elaborate on this later in this chapter.

2. The spiral process of narrative learning

The question we have been trying to address in this book is in what way narratives can enhance the kind of learning defined above. So far, we have proposed that narrative is an avenue by which we can understand better our lived experience as persons and imagine ourselves into and articulate the person we are to become. Some authors term this process self-authoring (McAdams, Josselson, & Lieblich, 2006). The metaphor of life as narrative and self-authoring is an attractive one because it enables individuals to enter another's life and way of being through a textual exchange. Thus Witherell (1995, pp. 40–41) writes:

> Narrative allows us to enter empathically into another's life and being—to join a living conversation. In this sense, it serves as a means of inclusion, inviting the reader, listener, writer, or teller as a companion along on another's journey. In the process we may find ourselves wiser, more receptive, more understanding, nurtured, and sometimes healed.

However, it can be problematic to see the person and his/her life as a text or a story because there is the danger of losing sight of human subjectivity and agency. Our capacity as humans to re-construct our personal narrative allows us to gain a more critical and interpretive perspective of our life and thereafter our actions and ways of being in the world. In this book, we suggest this is achieved through creating an all-encompassing space for hermeneutic interpretation and dialogic interaction, which is empowering and inspiring.

Narrative learning is also 'life learning', learning in/through the process of living, and it involves ongoing elaboration and modification of a person's life stories. Some people's narrative capacity and character allow them to be more reflexive and more open to shifting their stories for their own personal wellbeing and for a better vision of their life. Others may take a more fixed view of their life's course, in which case, their life story can become tyrannous, and the result is stasis or ossification rather than life learning.

Hence we have pointed out that it is important to detail this process of narration and interpretation in order to understand how dialogue about life events can change a person's understanding of the landscape within which his/her story is located. Life stories can change and adapt as life is lived, experienced and recounted. They can be modified by life events themselves, including new ideas encountered, new meanings engendered, new books read, new initiatives undertaken, new historical periods, new geographical locations, in short, by new circumstances. Modification as such can happen both with and without the stimulus of a deliberate and facilitating narrative process. Naturally, people can learn intuitively, especially those who are by nature more reflexive and have a strong narrative capacity. These are people who take any opportunity that life offers to reflect on experiences, shifts and meaning. A tendency to be reflexive does not guarantee that learning takes place. From what has been discussed so far, it is necessary to create a space for dialogic narrative encounter between people because that in itself is the beginning of narrative modification. We have illustrated this in both Christopher and George's cases. Hence, modification begins with new stimuli of this sort—these provide the opportunity to engender an additional life episode or new version of a life story.

However, each new stimulus will also encounter the existing narrative frame, so there is a process of reframing. Narrative learning includes some kind of negotiation, most often interior, conducted as an 'internal conversation' that a person has with him/herself, by which the 'new' is incorporated into the existing narrative frame. It may sound strange and intriguing to consider how a conversation can be had with oneself. The conversation is between the different 'voices' one has within oneself. A person acts upon different voices within him/herself and each of these voices holds a different authority over the individual. (See our dialogue on the community of voices in Chapter Four.) Some of these voices are ancestors, some belong to a particular profession or vocation, some speak in the voice of dominant social and political forces, some speak from the concern of, for instance, being a parent, a child, or a sibling; some come from a person's own ego, and some may be represented by a higher vision or from spiritual sources. These voices debate inside the person and command his/her narrative in accordance with the interlocutors, the spaces from which he/she speaks, and for what purposes. So, reframing starts from an internal negotiation with these different voices and results in a person's decision in terms of what constitutes his/her commanding voice at the time. This internal conversation can then lead to a shift of voice in the life story.

The shift of voices in oral work such as literature and life stories has been examined from the notion of refraction, which refers to the turning or bending of any wave, such as a light or sound wave, when it passes from one medium into another of a different density. This long quote from Allen (2002) gives a good explanation of how refraction works in narrative:

> Sight mediates and metonymically represents the aesthetic refraction of reality in verbal as well as visual arts. The eye performs a literal act of translation. For the body, the eye is both an opening and an organ. The lungs and stomach process what mouth and nose inhale; the eye performs a more complex operation: it filters the world both into the body and into consciousness. Light, color, and form are interpreted rather than digested, refracted through memory. Although both trained and biologically programmed, the eye is more subjective, more selective, than the internal organs. On the threshold between the self and the world, the eye blinks, redirects and refocuses its gaze. Whereas the ear, that other liminal organ, filters sound that it cannot generate, the eye that sees is also the object of perception. In its fictional representations, the eye figures for 'I', for the subject's ways of knowing the world. It functions as opaque reflector, transparent frame, transforming prism, passive receptor, active projector, or lens magnifying consciousness (p. 2).

Following the previous discussion of narrative modification and reframing, the new stimulus enters through the personal 'window' frame but is refracted in a similar way to a light wave as it enters a window, in a variety of directions. This is the refocusing, redirecting, and reinterpreting Allen describes above, and the self, or the 'I', both interprets and is the one being interpreted, and who projects and the one who is being projected. Indeed, Allen's analysis of fictional characters' 'reflexive gaze' points out that there is a need for constant re-visioning of the world that people inhabit and the individuals who enter the dialogic and reflexive process will inevitably be forced to take responsibility for the re-visions. It is an indefinite refraction.

The 'I' in the narrative construct is the integration of subject and object and makes narrative learning a spiral-like process, never ending, but with a forward and upward momentum. Whilst the person's life stories integrate shifts from the past, the present, to the future, he/she also unfolds the episodes to be (re)lived so that they are more in line with current understanding, beliefs and values. In early chapters of this book, we examined the temporal character of life narrative. Now with the metaphor of refraction, it is possible to see how the individual can inter-pret and understand the narrative structure from different perspectives. For instance, with the support of an interlocutor, a facilitator, a critical friend, or a collaborator (which are different possible names for the partner in the dialogic exchange), one can focus on questions as follows:

a. Why are these stories told in this way at a particular time? Are there any themes emerging? How do the themes connect to each other?
b. What is the central plot of the narrative? Is it helpful in creating some kind of coherence in the person's life? If it does, how does he/she see the contradictions and gaps in his/her stories?
c. In whose voices are these stories told?

These questions allow narrative learning to be rigorous and holistic. In addi-tion, the interpretation of the narrative from multiple perspectives further gener-ates conversations and exchanges that bring in other dimensions of human experience—the socio-cultural, the historical, the political, and the personal. Narrative learning helps distinguish an identity that is inherited from ancestors, cul-tures, nation, ethnicity, gender, or derived from an upbringing within a commu-nity from an identity that is subject to social, religious, political and other power dynamics, as well as from a sense of oneself that is more autonomous and endur-ing. By taking a rigorous approach to narrative interpretation and meaning-mak-ing, narrative learning can be emancipatory and can unfold the dominant forces that shape the way a person constructs his/her narrative. This is not to suggest that a process like this can truly liberate one from diverse constraints and influences. However, an awareness of the multiple landscapes within a person's own narrative terrain can nevertheless empower them to begin to choose a life trajectory more in tune with his/her own nature, identity and perception of his/her purpose in the world.

Narrative learning has transformative potential, yet transformation does not mean a constant shift in an individual's narratives. In fact, narrative learning also seeks to consolidate a person's journeys and allow them to develop a sense of integrity in their overall narrative, uniting past and present experiences and formu-lating a future trajectory. This kind of consolidation is not in conflict with an over-all transformative agenda.

3. Expanding on narrative pedagogy

In this book, we put forward the notion of narrative encounters and suggest that education endeavours ought to be focused on facilitating dialogue and deep personal engagement through narrative exchange. Therefore, it is crucial for us to define and expand on the notion of pedagogy in order to work towards a theory of narrative pedagogy.

Pedagogy is defined as 'the art, occupation, or practice of teaching. Also the theory or principles of education; a method of teaching based on such a theory' (*Oxford English Dictionary*). Its etymology suggests that the original meaning be 'to lead the child' or 'to guide the learner'. It was from the Greek paidagogos, which means to lead from; to lead/guide. The concept of pedagogy has been criticised by many scholars for being interpreted as focusing on instruction and content-based teaching, power and authoritarianism. For instance, in Chapter Two of Paulo Freire's *Pedagogy of the Oppressed* (1970), the author listed the following 'pedagogic principles' that underpin what he termed a 'banking' model of education that aims at oppressing the people:

a. the teacher teaches and the students are taught;

b. the teacher knows everything and the students know nothing;

c. the teacher thinks and the students are thought about;

d. the teacher talks and the students listen—meekly;

e. the teacher disciplines and the students are disciplined;

f. the teacher chooses and enforces his choice, and the students comply;

g. the teacher acts and the students have the illusion of acting through the action of the teacher;

h. the teacher chooses the program content, and the students (who were not consulted) adapt to it;

i. the teacher confuses the authority of knowledge with his or her own professional authority, which she or he sets in opposition to the freedom of the students;

j. the teacher is the subject of the learning process, while the students are mere objects.

In a climate where education is being conceptualised instrumentally in many societies, no wonder the notion of pedagogy suffers from such a negative connotation. Therefore in this book, we want to reclaim the importance of pedagogy as a set of principles underpinning educative activities, and highlight the noble work that teachers and educators do in order to enable and guide the learners' learning.

For us, pedagogy is more than principles of instruction. We define narrative pedagogy as the facilitation of an educative journey through which learning takes place in profound encounters, and by engaging in meaning-making and deep dialogue and exchange.

We propose a framework of narrative pedagogy consisting in four key elements:

a.   teacher's authentic engagement including sharing personal narratives,

b.   deep caring relationships,

c.   respect, and

d.   love.

Narrative pedagogy starts with teachers' authentic engagement. Parker Palmer writes, 'good teaching cannot be reduced to technique; good teaching comes from the identity and integrity of the teacher' (1998, p. 10). Palmer then goes on to articulate what he means by those two important notions.

> By *identity* I mean an evolving nexus where all the forces that constitute my life converge in the mystery of self: my genetic makeup, the nature of the man and woman who gave me life, the culture in which I was raised, people who have sustained me and people who have done me harm, the good and ill I have done to others and to myself, the experience of love and suffering—and much, much more. In the midst of that complex field, identity is a moving intersection of the inner and outer forces that make me who I am, converging in the irreducible mystery of being human.

> By *integrity* I mean whatever wholeness I am able to find within that nexus as its vectors form and re-form the pattern of my life. Integrity requires that I discern what is integral to my selfhood, what fits and what does not—and that I choose life-giving ways of relating to the forces that converge within me: Do I welcome them or fear them, embrace them or reject them, move with them or against them? By choosing integrity, I become more whole, but wholeness does not mean perfection. It means becoming more real by acknowledging the whole of who I am (*ibid.*, p. 13).

The mystery of self is at the centre of education and learning because good teaching starts from there, and ultimately, the mystery of being human is reflected in the teacher's narrative. This makes narrative exchange the precondition of pedagogy because learning is about becoming.

Narrative pedagogy also involves deep relationships. In Chapter Five, we discussed how the narrative process is a whole-person encounter that involves emotion, intuition, and the human spirit. The relationship between the teacher and the learner is the key to narrative learning. Noddings (2010) claims that relationship is ontologically basic. 'Human beings are born from and into relation; it is our original condition' (p. 390), and that approaching the world through a caring relation:

> we are more likely to listen attentively to others. In a caring relation, the carer is first of all attentive to the cared-for, and this attention is receptive; that is the carer puts aside her own values and projects, and tries to understand the expressed needs of the cared-for (p. 391).

In Noddings' terms, the carer is a teacher, and the cared-for, the learner. This withdrawing of the teacher's values in order to attend to the projects of the learner is a non-judgmental approach to the learner's narrative, which does not exclude the opportunity for the teacher to attend to what in the learner's narrative is at odds with his/her own perspectives. We don't see that Noddings' claim here contradicts Gadamer's view of integrating bias that arises from one's tradition and horizons in the process of understanding the other, reviewed in Chapter Five. This is because by putting aside temporarily the teacher's own projects, he/she focuses on the learner's needs and projects in order to maintain a caring relationship. Meanwhile, to evaluate and respond to a wide range of needs expressed by the learner, the teacher 'must expand the breadth of her competence' (*ibid.,* p. 391). Noddings suggests that to complete the relationship, the learner must recognise the teacher's effort as *caring*. She writes:

> The response of the cared-for is an act of reciprocity, but it is not the contractual reciprocity so familiar to us in traditional Western philosophy. The cared-for usually cannot do for the carer what the carer can do for the cared-for, nor must he promise payment of some kind. The act of recognition is itself a form of reciprocity—completing the relation and providing confirmatory evidence that the carer is on the right track (*ibid.*).

Relationship is an interplay involving giving and taking (Hayden, 1980). In facilitating narrative learning, the teacher and the learner both share their understanding, knowledge, worldviews, values and personal experiences. Through such giving and sharing, the teacher and the learners themselves mutually enrich each other's humanity (Hayden, 1995).

Relationship and reciprocity in pedagogy do not necessarily require equal treatment or consistency because individuals respond to each other and their narratives differently. However, it does require the teacher undertaking to reach out to the learners in a caring and sensitive way. By caring, the pedagogue can identify the opportunity, when it arises, for the learners to reflect on their narrative and to use it as a basis to develop their individual qualities and to direct their lives.

Narrative pedagogy is an invitation to enter another individual's mind, emotions and spirit as well as values, worldviews, traditions, and moral and personal dilemmas. Narrative pedagogy is about showing respect and appreciation for an individual's nature, disposition, talents and aspiration. It also depends on the teacher's ability to identify with the learners as persons and fellow human beings, and to be open to the learners' self-knowledge, current needs, narrative capacities and characters, lived experience of the past and present, and their capacities for consolidating, modifying and transforming their narratives towards their wellbeing and flourishing.

Some scholars have linked relationship, care and respect to the notion of love in its broadest sense, which is the giving of self, not only arising from compassion, but also coming from higher sources. This places pedagogy within the realm of a profoundly ethical endeavour which ultimately concerns enabling individuals to live life fully and meaningfully and to achieve what we have called 'integrity'.

Pedagogy is a moral activity (Carr, 2000). This is because whatever choices are made, there are moral implications. The teacher's choices of acting in a particular way in her teaching, for example, deciding to share personal narratives, to enter a reciprocal relationship with the learner, to show respect and love to the learners in her group. These are based on moral decisions. There are also moral elements behind other day-to-day decisions and choices people make. To a great extent, the pedagogical focus in facilitating narrative learning is to provide a safe space for both the teacher and the learner to examine the ethical decisions that confront the individual in his everyday personal and social life and to examine what kind of person or human being one would like to become.

Narrative pedagogy ultimately respects human dignity and, as Parker Palmer points out, aims to help individuals to 'discern what is integral' to their personhood and make choices about what constitutes their integrity so that each becomes whole.

4. Facilitating the narrative learning process

In Chapter Five, we described the dialogic and collaborative process for developing personal narrative. The process contains a spiral of construction and reconstruction in a cycle of narration, collaboration and location which also consists of theorisation and integration (see Figure 2). The sequences form a spiral which is a continual and ongoing intense process. In our early discussions, this process was perceived from the perspective of life history research. Having explored pedagogy and the role of the teacher, we now explain how this narrative process can be facilitated by an educator, a teacher.

As shown in Figure 2, the starting point is creating a space for narration. Our experience is that it is always helpful to provide an opportunity for the learner to reflect on his/her life stories before the narration. In this way, narration has a pre-active phase and an interactive phase. A timeline is a useful aid for the pre-active phase or preparation as are drawings, artefacts, and metaphors. We have to trust people's creative capacities to use what appeals to them. Over time, we have seen many fantastic ideas, such as writing one's life as a personal myth, drawings one's life as a journey or a river, colour-coded timelines, and the use of objects and memorabilia.

To facilitate narrative learning, time for preparation is a crucial reflective process when the learner begins to ask questions such as 'Who am I?', 'How have I become?', 'What are the major events in my life?' and many more. The pre-active phase covers the engendering of new events and stimuli through to framing refraction and narrative incorporation. It is vitally important at the narration stage that the teacher or educator also shares her own narrative. This gesture places the teacher/education as an equal participant of this process rather than an expert or voyeur.

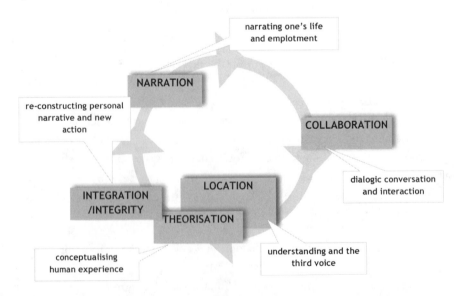

Figure 2: Spiral process of narrative learning

Following on from narration is a collaborative event where stories and interpretations are exchanged and reconstructed and revisited. Collaboration can also take place in a group social setting—where the participants (the teacher/facilitator and the learners) compare their stories and interpretation, develop thematic and conceptual understandings and insights, and identify challenges and dilemmas. Collaboration can also take place in a sense with texts—documents and readings which can have the same collaborative effect as face-to-face meetings, if less animated.

Collaboration often appears to be chaotic as the teacher/facilitator and her group enter the narrative 'maze' of a person. We use the metaphor of maze to describe the often competing meanings and understandings of events that the narrator assumes in his/her own narration. The sorting out and ordering of events, although carefully thought through, might not have been presented by the narrator in ways that reflect his/her understanding, or may appear to not fully address the narrator's struggles and dilemmas. This depends on each person's narrative capacities and narrative character as discussed earlier. The key is to trust that at the end of this collaborative endeavour, new understanding of one's life and new interpretations of events can be achieved as a result of intense conversation, dialogue, questioning, negotiating meaning and critical collaborative interpretation. This is often when the most extended discussion and debate takes place and therefore the most chaotic part of the process.

One way for the facilitator (educator/teacher) to lead a group through such a narrative maze is intense listening as proposed by John Dewey in what he termed 'listening–in–conversation'. Waks (2010, p. 5) defines such listening as transactional listening and writes:

> This distinct kind of listening is not understood in terms of separate, fixed poles of speaker and listener, ready-made speaker contents, and even ready-made vocabularies. As he (Dewey) puts it, "When A and B carry on a conversation together the action is a trans-action: both are concerned in it; its results pass, as it were, across from one to the other", an image that suggests electrical currents that connect the two poles in a single circuit. In this *connected* form of listening the receptive sides of the transactions are also active and aim-directed, and the active sides are also receptive. The listening is *constructive*, in that the participants, their communication contents, and even their very vocabularies, are all constructed or re-constructed in conversational give and take.
>
> . . .
>
> Dewey construes humans as living creatures who, by virtue of prior biological and social conditioning, seek new enjoyments and renewals in each transaction.

Intense listening allows the facilitator and others in the group to enter the same circuit of narrative encounter and to enter the reciprocal relationship we discussed earlier in this chapter. In this way, listening-in-conversation allows the narrative to be co-constructed in the conversation and collaboration. Thus the key to facilitation is to encourage intense listening and for the teacher/facilitator to model intense listening too.

It is essential that the facilitator respects the learners' stories, but also maintains an ability to look beyond the learners' initial stories in order to help them to understand themselves and their experience more deeply. The educator/facilitator's caring attitude and close relationship with the learners can ensure that the collaboration provides an ideal leverage for narrative learning. This would be achieved through the educator/facilitator's willingness to take risks by inviting open dialogue amongst the learners and him/herself, and his/her aptitude for asking good questions and listening deeply that goes beyond only hearing what was narrated, to 'hearing' what is unsaid (See Palmer, 1998). This is about teaching from one's identity and integrity (*ibid.*).

In agreeing with Palmer, what we have termed 'integrity' is a sense of the universal, the holistic. It is where a sense of selfhood is 'located' in time and space and understood in its full perspective and meaningfulness. The building of the episodic bridges to the universal is one of the major pedagogic routes to be explored in the process of narrative learning.

Through collaboration, the learners come to locate their own narrative in historical, cultural and social spaces. Location provides a degree of understanding as to why individuals tell their story in this way at this moment. Human stories are a personal elaboration and construction, but the 'building' bricks and sometimes the elementary parts of narrative scripts are socially located. Stories also integrate the characteristics of particular historical periods into this ongoing process of narrative 'bricolage', i.e., made from a variety of bits and bobs of experience. Location involves a process of coming to know the importance of time and social forces as they impinge on a person's stories. In a sense, the individual cannot fully know what is 'personal', what has been refracted until he/she comes to understand their stories' historical and social locations. Location then, is a highly pedagogic process and, as with collaboration, provides a variety of pedagogic levers for the lifelong learner.

However, seeking pedagogical moments for the learner to grow and transform does not necessarily mean an ongoing shift in a person's narrative. At this juncture, the teacher/facilitator must show trust in the learner's capacity to pursue further goals in terms of narrative and actions. This means that the teacher/facilitator accepts that a person's life is after all his own responsibility. They rework their life bearing in mind the basic reality of existence, time, and possibility of mortality.

Note that this is not a 'stage' theory or a hierarchical pattern but rather an endless spiral. People join at different points of the cycle and move in a spiral manner, revisiting themes or experiences. Some life stories move into theorisation: a more abstract understanding of a person's stories, which is a bridge between what has been reflected, philosophised and articulated and his or her own life. This transition can provide a take-off point for developing a strategic approach to living a good life (which for us is in the Aristotelian sense) or articulating an integral narration where the person presents a holistic sense of themselves, and assumes a direction in life that shows their integrity. Our sense is that moving through location, theorising and integrity are the points at which narrative learning may become transformative. Transformative in the sense that one can now begin to live an examined life (in the words of Socrates), a good life. But we stress that integrity is not the final end point—it is a point on the journey. New conditions and transitions begin the spiral of learning once again.

One way to understand the transformative process of theorising a life and developing an ecological sense of selfhood is by an analogy with grieving. In both processes a person has to come to a more detached (theorised) view of his/her situation and in the process of acceptance develops a more holistic sense of his/her personal vision. We saw this process at work with a number of the life storytellers in our research and teaching experience as they came to the later stages of their lives. In Christopher's process, for instance, as detailed in Chapter Four, he began to understand his own life story in a new way as he came to terms with his own mortality. In a sense he is grieving for his heroic self, the self that carved out a life project in the face of childhood trauma. As well as grieving he is coming to a new acceptance of life. It is an acceptance that life could be lived without the overwhelming and commanding voice that had dominated his inner conversation for the majority of his life. This was the voice of his childhood fears and monstrous self-blame. Through location and theorisation he came to see the limits of his overarching individual narrative and to craft a new and holistic vision of selfhood.

Whilst a pattern of selfhood is being deconstructed with acceptance, a new narrative of selfhood begins to emerge. In this sense 'acceptance' becomes a major pedagogic threshold. Often, acceptance is linked to an understanding that private, individual issues are part of broader human concerns. This linking of the individual to the wider 'common stream' of humanity moves a person's narrative forward. The reconciliation moves through two milieu: firstly, the reconciliation with each individual's own personal stories and psychic landscapes, a process of coming to accept who we are, and why we have storied the world in the way we have; and secondly, a broader sense of reconciliation with the wider world and the multi-faceted human condition.

What we must stress though is the episodic nature of narrative pedagogy and learning. Life throws up many challenges and transitions, dilemmas and disorientations, changes and continuities; meanwhile the wider historical and social context is subject to similar disruptions, dysfunctions and conjectures. As a result, the spiral of narrative pedagogy and learning is in endless flux. Moments of integrity are followed by moments of ambiguity, moments of transformation by moments of consolidation. This is a process of endlessly 'returning to go'—each time the learning threshold has been built at a new level—the process of being and becoming is therefore, for many, cumulative. It is a sort of upward 'ratchet' effect. The purpose of narrative pedagogy is to maximise this cumulative process in ways that facilitate human meaning-making and human happiness.

5. Jennie—a case study of the narrative process

Jennie was in her early fifties when Scherto's conversation with her began. Jennie was part of a wider study exploring the impact of narrative encounter on individuals' understanding of themselves, their life and their actions in the world. Scherto and Jennie's conversation continued over a period of one year during which they met four times, each meeting lasting two to three hours.

Jennie is a district nurse, and a team leader. Jennie and her team provide healthcare and medical treatment to elderly people in a county council in England. Many of the elderly either suffer from long term illnesses or are terminally ill. Jennie's job involves visiting the elderly in care homes or their own homes.

Born in a middle-class family, Jennie's father was a musician, head of a music college in England; her mother was a school teacher and then a deputy headteacher. She also has two siblings—one elder sister who is 'the beautiful one' and who is married to a rich businessman and has been living in the USA for the last thirty-five years, and one younger brother who suffers from schizophrenia.

Jennie said that throughout her childhood, she was under tremendous pressure to do well. Her father tried to teach her to play the piano when she was four or five years old, but Jennie said that she didn't have enough talent, which was a 'huge disappointment' to her father. Then she was encouraged to try another instrument—the violin, taught by a well-known violinist and a family friend. Although she wasn't keen on either instrument, Jennie was not allowed to give up without trying. So by the time she was fourteen, she only achieved Grade Five in both. That was after at least eight years' practice. She was finally given permission by her parents to discontinue with her music lessons.

Jennie attended the junior school where her mother was the deputy head. She put in a lot of effort to help Jennie prepare for the Eleven Plus exams. Unfortunately, Jennie didn't pass and said that she felt sick on the exam days out of nervousness and pressure. So this was another occasion where she felt to have failed 'hopelessly'. Jennie lost the opportunity to go to a grammar school and with it any hope of academic success then and since.

Parallel to the academic failure stories, was Jennie's other storyline where she was a popular girl amongst her contemporaries and had solid friendships with her peers. Throughout the conversation, Jennie appears to recognise that she is 'naturally very good with people', and that she is able to get on well with anyone, children, adults and people from all works of life. She was the only one in the family who could relate to the youngest schizophrenic child. Jennie still visits him regularly as an adult and takes good care of him.

Yet, failing academically remained as a strong thread in Jennie's narrative. She constantly refers to it. This thread and the one about her interest in human wellbeing and her ability to relate to people easily, formed two important contexts for building up her main story—a story of being a nurse and of being caring.

Not having any confidence in doing well academically, as Jennie puts it, she left school at the age of sixteen with five GCSEs including one in English, her favourite subject at school. She spent a couple of years' travelling while working in pubs and cafes to support herself. After this break, she decided to train as a nurse, and she has been working as a nurse ever since. When Scherto asked why she trained in nursing, Jennie's initial response was that nursing didn't require any academic work as it is more hands-on.

Over the years, Jennie has tried really hard to improve her own skills and expand her knowledge as a nursing professional. She is always eager to learn new things and is an avid reader. Jennie now has acquired senior nursing qualification; she is an NLP (Neuro Linguistic Programming) therapist, a qualified counsellor, and hypnotherapist. She also practises yoga and meditation and intends to take a spiritual approach to helping the elderly, in particular those who are terminally ill. In her work, Jennie does her best to help them and their family prepare for the journey leading to death and help the surviving relatives learn to live through their grief.

Jennie is not married and has no children but lives with a long term partner who is a craftsman. They have been together since they were seventeen. In her spare time, Jennie reads a lot, and helps young lone mothers. She is godmother to a little boy, Zak, born to a young woman who was living in a hostel for the homeless.

The two women met when Jennie was volunteering at the hostel one Christmas. Jennie helped with Zak's delivery. Since then, she has been a mentor, friend and positive influence on the young woman who is now a qualified hairdresser and is raising Zak independently. Jennie said that she didn't want to have children of her own as there are enough children in the world for her to love and care for. A close relationship with Zak fulfils her motherhood needs.

Scherto and Jennie's conversational collaboration focused on the notion of academia and what it meant for each of them. Scherto shared her story as an academic and how she thrives on being a researcher and academic author. Jennie, on the contrary, regards academia as an exclusive and alienating world. Scherto shared her observation that to her, Jennie appears to be highly articulate and thoughtful. Her reflexivity and profound insights into her own work and life show high degree of intellectual capacity. These conversations made Jennie realise, with some reluctance, that her enrichment studies and training in higher qualification in healthcare management, NLP course and counselling qualification could all be considered academic.

These conversations formed the basis for them to collaborate and to locate Jennie's story of academic failure within a broader educational system that is obsessed with exam results and intellectual achievements and which takes these as the only measures for 'success'. In Jennie's words, 'it totally ignores the student as a whole person, and neglects the diversity of human talents'.

In their later conversation, Jennie explains her change of attitude:

> I have never linked what I do with anything academic and certainly had never perceived myself in the light of an intellectual. Perhaps it is all right now for me not to be too dismissive about academia. The term is very narrow any way, and the connotation it has simply puts many people off. Like you said, it is not the intellectual way of thinking that I am up against. Academia was a curse for me for many years. It always has an element of ticking the right box about something totally irrelevant to what I really care about. But in fact, it can be really stimulating. I have to say that I wouldn't have enjoyed the NLP course that much if there hadn't been the literature about neurological processes, human behavioral patterns, and writings about the way our language determines our thoughts, etc. As you say, it is highly intellectual content and I love reading books of such intellectual weight. So I might be more open to intellectual stuff but I will never consider myself to be an academic, at least, not for the sake of being one.

This conversation also had unexpected effect on Jennie's understanding of her vocational choice, and the kind of life she has lived so far:

For a long time, I have agreed with my parents that it was due to the early failure in academia that I have chosen a more hands-on vocation of nursing. Now I am not so sure. You know what, I really think that if I had been successful academically, I would still have chosen it. I remember when I was in training, someone asked me: 'You are so competent, have you thought about training to become a doctor?' At the time, my answer was 'Oh, I can't bear the academic stuff.' Looking back, I know now that I wouldn't have wanted to be a doctor because it doesn't allow me to have such interaction with people that I care for.

. . .

Nursing suits me best. I love looking after people, especially those who are vulnerable and helpless. It is nothing to do with wanting to be a saviour or a hero. I do know some social workers share that kind of mentality. I love nursing because I believe everyone deserves dignity in their life, and nursing and healthcare is an important way to help maintain people's dignity. So that's what I'm meant to be doing—a life's mission, if you like. It is what I found most meaningful and hugely rewarding too. You see, what I offer to the people is often returned generously. They return it with respect, appreciation, a loving attitude towards me, and there is of course, friendship. I can't imagine any other work that would allow me to express so deeply my own beliefs and what I commit myself to.

Have you heard of compassion in healthcare? It sounds like a new buzz word, but what it says is that it is important to integrate the human dimension in healthcare. It doesn't have to be complicated. Someone defines it as the humane quality of understanding suffering in others and wanting to do something about it. It is the kind of quality that comes naturally to children. Many of us in nursing do it. For instance, it can be really simple things such as holding the person's hand when you talk to them or really listen to them; not treating the person in front of us as just a 'patient', but seeing them as someone whom we could help improve their life's quality. It is a bit like the pedagogy you are talking about—what I do is to facilitate a process where the persons are empowered to re-claim their dignity.

Re-reading Jennie's narrative and Scherto's conversations with her, Jennie and Scherto both agreed that the narrative encounter between them resulted in a consolidation of Jennie's long held beliefs and values. It is also transformative not in the sense of a dramatic change but through developing her professional and personal integrity. Jennie concluded that the narrative exchange had enabled her to understand that there is little division between her work as a nurse and her life as a person. She was content that she is able to lead a life of such integrity and shall continue to do so.

6. Dialogue and reflection

Scherto: In this chapter, our focus is on developing narrative pedagogy. We realised that it is not an easy task to show how the process of facilitation is carried out in a small space such as this book, nevertheless we chose Jennie's narrative as a case study to give an example of how her voice shifts as the result of the dialogic interaction. Do you think through this excerpt, we were able to give the reader a flavour of the working of narrative pedagogy?

Ivor: Yes, and no. Your conversation with Jennie hinges on the so-called 'academic failure' which seems to have occupied a big space in her narration. The reason that the theme was attractive to you was because of the kind of background you came from and the kind of interest you have in academia. If it were another person who is interested in music or who is interested in healthcare issues, the conversation between Jennie and the other interlocutor may have zoomed in on a different focus. This shows that narrative pedagogy is not to be detached from the identity and authenticity of the educator/facilitator as we have claimed earlier. So in this sense, it does give the reader a flavour.

Ivor: It hasn't worked in terms of exhibiting the process of narrative pedagogy. The excerpt does not offer any insight into how deep listening is, and how the two of you went through the chaotic process of collaboration and the strenuous exchange trying to locate the narrative within a broader historical and political context of British education. Neither does your excerpt give the reader a sense of how the broad pathology we tentatively put forward in this chapter might work in a pedagogical intervention.

Scherto: If I can just add to that. It also worked because from the way Jennie reflected on her own identity and her agency, there seems to emerge a 'third voice' which we also addressed earlier. The third voice highlights the shift in our perception and understanding through the collaborative endeavour. What emerges is the 'fusion of horizons' which moves beyond the singular voices of us two interlocutors. So through narrative pedagogy, a new understanding is developed which is more than the sum of the two separate parts. So my sense is that it has worked in terms of the new voice. But where hasn't it worked to offer a flavour of the narrative pedagogy?

Scherto: It does, however, show how our narrative encounter allowed us to immediately lock into apparently fluent narrative flows and have a very intense and thematically rich interchange on the topic of 'academia'. They provided a rich ground for the development of the third voice. This further gave us an opportunity to arrive at a place where her abstract thinking led to her awareness of her own integrity in life and work.

Ivor: But other narrative encounters are much more sparse and sporadic with only occasional patches of thematic intensity and richness. In these instances the collaborative progress starts from a different place and therefore develops in a different way.

Scherto: Given the thematic intensity in my conversations with Jennie, she and I still travelled a long winding journey in the conversation. In fact, it was a deep experience for me too. A brief excerpt does not allow the reader to see the new insights that I developed in understanding my own narrative and about education. This reminds me of a colleague, Laura Formenti, who once said to me: 'The process of helping the learners or participants arrive at their own narrative is like the process of giving birth, and narrative educators are like the midwives.' I might go one step further to suggest that both the educator and the learner are to give 'birth' to new narratives.

Questions for discussion

Our main task for this chapter is two-fold: to clarify our definition of learning and to develop the theory of narrative pedagogy. For the former, we focused our conception of learning on human development including nurturing those qualities and virtues necessary for being and becoming more human. For the latter, we propose a framework consisting of four elements: teacher's identity and integrity in their authentic engagement, deep and caring relationship, respect and love in the broadest sense.

We also illustrated the process of facilitating narrative learning by offering a spiral process of narrative stages and their relevance for learning and pedagogy. In terms of the nature of narrative learning, we pointed out that sometimes the focus of pedagogy can be transformative and at other times consolidatory. Narrative pedagogy respects these different movements in the individual's narrative and learning journeys.

The case study of Jennie's narrative journey prompted several questions which we ourselves have already raised and discussed. Other questions remain:

- Within the proposed framework for narrative pedagogy, what other elements might we have forgotten that are crucial for the facilitation of learning?
- What are the situations where narrative pedagogy can apply?
- We reintroduced the notion of the 'third voice' which is crucial in enhancing each person's understanding of themselves and developing their agency. How does narrative pedagogy encourage the 'third voice'?
- The conversation between Scherto and Jennie also happens in everyday life between friends and colleagues. Does it mean that anyone can facilitate narrative learning?

Suggested Reading

Cohler, B. J., & Cole, T. R. (1996). Studying older lives: Reciprocal acts of telling and listening. In J. E. Birren & G. M. Kenyon (Eds.), *Aging and biography: Explorations in adult development* (pp. 61–76). New York: Springer.

Dominicé, P. (2000). *Learning from our lives: Using educational biographies with adults.* San Francisco: Jossey-Bass.

McLaughlin, D., & Tierney, W. (Eds.). (1993). *Naming silenced lives: Personal narratives and the process of educational change.* New York: Routledge.

Munro, P. (1998). *Subject to fiction: Women teachers' life history narratives and the cultural politics of resistance.* London: Open University Press.

Noddings, N. (1991). Stories in dialogue. In C. Witherall & N. Noddings (Eds.), *Stories lives tell: Narrative and dialogue in education.* New York: Teachers College Press.

8

Narrative: Learning and Living in the Community

Our lives are ceaselessly intertwined with narrative, with the stories that we tell and hear told, those we dream or imagine or would like to tell, all of which are reworked in that story of our own lives that we narrate to ourselves in an episodic, sometimes semi-conscious, but virtually uninterrupted monologue. We live immersed in narrative, recounting and reassessing the meaning of our past actions, anticipating the outcome of our future projects, situating ourselves at the intersection of several stories not yet completed.

Peter Brooks, *Reading for the Plot: Design and Intention in Narrative,* 1984

Introduction

After examining narrative as a research methodology and investigating its potential as a pedagogic site for learning, this book has thus far tried to established a theory of narrative pedagogy.

There are three things that this final chapter will aim to do.

First, we return to the conceptual bases and the methodological challenges of narrative that we examined in the first part of the book; and review the reflexive nature of narrative learning and pedagogy explored in the second part of the book. We extend our exploration further into the realm of morality and ethics. By working collaboratively on people's existing narrative, memories and understanding, we claim that it can help change the way that individuals, groups and communities interact and co-exist in society. Narrative reconstruction is therefore not only an individual process of revisiting and re-organising our stories of the self, including our sense of moral being, but also provides a basis for groups and communities to reflect on and consolidate their sense of integrity and wellbeing.

Next, we bring our discussion of narrative to focus on the social process of identity development, agency, human actions and engagement. We want to examine this by using the example of narrative learning within a group context in teacher education.

Lastly, we look at the wider implications of narrative pedagogy and narrative learning in other settings, including collective memories, narrative learning in forgiveness work and conflict transformation, reminiscence work and so forth.

1. Narrative understanding, agency and social action

At the beginning of the book where we reviewed the definition and the nature of narrative, we suggested there is something fundamentally human about the notion of narrative. It is an important tool for humans to make sense of life as lived and to use this understanding in order to examine and guide ongoing human experiences. This new understanding is represented by what we call a 'third voice'. To arrive at the new insight, we have said that it requires an intimate relationship and an intense process of narrative encounter—encountering the 'other' on many different levels, including the other of oneself that is not yet familiar and known.

To understand and analyse this difference in narrative encounters it is important to distinguish between the *pre-active* narrative process, the *interactive* narrative encounter and the *post-interactive* reflection and narrative *re-construction*—what we call the *afterlife* (of narrative process). It is our contention that the pre-active narrative character of the participant (in a narrative and life history research setting), or the learner (in a pedagogical context), or the interlocutor (in everyday conversational situations) is a crucial variable in the thematic richness and indeed the pedagogic or transformative potential that is present. Narrative pedagogy through facilitating narrative encounter, therefore, first and foremost, needs to be acutely sensitive to these pre-active narrative characteristics.

During the interactive narrative encounter, we pointed out the importance of qualities such as caring, respect, relationships and dignity in the dialogic processes. Listening, in particular, deep listening, is the key to enable the individual to arrive at new insights and new understanding as well as emotions, empathy, intuition, compassion and imagination. These qualities anchor human narratives within values, ethics and worldviews. Post-interactive reflection is like the afterlife of the narrative encounter. Long after the narrative interactive encounter is over, the participant goes on processing and reflecting on what has taken place during that interchange.

The discussion of distinctive narrative capacities has to be understood within the overall position of narrative knowledge itself. One of the difficulties of writing about narratives as knowledge is where this knowledge has been located in Western societies. Bruner (1985, 1990) argued that there are two dominant paradigms of knowledge: the logico-scientific form of knowledge, which he calls paradigmatic cognition and the narrative form of knowledge or narrative cognition. Much of learning theory and curriculum theory works with the grain of the logico-scientific form. Hence, to move to a scrutiny of narrative knowledge, or in our words, narrative understanding, we have to develop the philosophical and sociological underpinnings of a new way of knowing.

Paradigmatic cognition works at a certain level of abstraction and de-contextualisation, by classifying events as belonging to categories or concepts and establishing connections between these categories and concepts. Individuals exist as belonging to categories and are conceptualised by the qualities such categories have in common. Such classifications can be elicited by quantitative surveys as well as other hypothesis-testing devices of the logico-scientific mode.

Narrative cognition works altogether differently, acknowledging that human agency and action emerge from the interaction between a person's previous learning and experience (their pro-active narrative), their present-situated context and their future-oriented purposes and objectives. Narrative cognition does not separate the rational, emotional and other ways of knowing. It is more holistic, involving the whole person.

Furthermore, narrative cognition also involves the process whereby humans come to understand the structural and chronological coherence of an individually-located story. Czarniawska defines the genre of narrative cognition par excellence, the life story as a 'narrative of individual history [that] is placed in a narrative of social history' (2004, p. 5). We call this the process of developing an individual narrative within a 'theory of context', or historical 'location'. The person comes to understand his or her own story alongside the elements of social construction that reside in any historical setting.

If we accept that narrative cognition has been under-represented at least in Western societies and subordinated to the promotion of paradigmatic cognition, we should argue for the vigorous rehabilitation of life narrative. Narrative then should be placed at the centre of pedagogic endeavour, and it behooves us to understand how pre-active life stories are themselves configured in different ways before being subsequently consolidated or reconfigured.

Narrative has provided humans with a profound reflective and interpretive framework for holding together lived experience, tensions, shifts and continuity. Whether it is research dilemma, or pedagogy for personal development, narrative goes beyond a set of procedures which can be simply followed. Rather, it creates opportunities for encountering on many levels including sharing individual struggles, emotions and motivation. Given the human variables involved in the pedagogic encounters, as we have persistently argued, these cannot be proceduralised. Sometimes the process is quite orderly almost routine, and other times it becomes messy even chaotic. This is evitable given the nature of encounter and the aspiration involved.

In Chapter One, we reviewed briefly MacIntyre's (1984) work which helped us to understand the ways narrative makes it possible for humans to explain and unify actions and identify the individuals' places within the wider historical settings where they belong. So we concluded in our early chapter of this book:

> This consolidates a mutually constitutive relationship between life and narrative— life forms the fundamental basis of narrative and narrative provides order, structure and direction in life, and helps develop meanings in richer and more integrated ways (Chapter Two).

The narrative pedagogy we put forward further places human narrative and selfhood within the realm of ethics. Schweiker (2004, p. 14) writes about the need for ethics in the context of what he calls 'globality':

> "Globality," an intensive awareness of the world as a whole, was lately born from the bloody political, ethnic, economic, and colonial conflicts of the twentieth century. Who among us does not sense the acceleration and even confusion of life?

While considering the challenges that humanity faces, Schweiker further maintains that what is at risk is human integrity:

> The age of globalization is one in which all forms of life—from molecular structures to rain forests—are intimately bound to the expansion and use of human power. What is now threatened is the integrity of life (p. 16).

So the question is, what kind of response should humans offer to the new situation in order to continue advancing human wellbeing and flourishing and, at the same time, ensure that the world around us remains sustainable.

In this book, we address this concern for human agency from the perspective of ethics and propose that seeking an ethical response to the challenges confronting human beings is the foremost task of the global era. What we mean by 'ethical' is about what it is to be good, as well as what is right to do for the individuals as well as for the wider community. Like Charles Taylor, Schweiker sees that the closeness of humans and the expansion of human consciousness provides fertile moral spaces for negotiating meaning, but most importantly, 'reasons for actions rather than causes of events' (2004, p. 22).

The way narrative encounter and dialogic exchange works towards individual self-examination and moral interrogation is not new. Authors quoted in this book such as MacIntyre, Ricoeur, Charles Taylor and others have already prepared a solid philosophical ground for a connection between narrative and the moral self. According to these authors, moral principles and ethics cannot be detached from human narratives because if moral principles are to be established, they are to be found within a narrative construction of human life. This refers back to our earlier citation of MacIntyre's, who suggested that humans are essentially storytelling animals. He writes:

> man is in his action and practice, as well as in his fictions, essentially a story-telling animal. He is not essentially, but becomes through his history, a teller of stories that aspire for truth (1984, p. 216)

One reading of this is that human integrity is about the harmony between a person's life as narrated, his/her sense of selfhood as expressed in the narrative, and his/her actions in the world.

2. Biographies in teacher education—learning within a community

Dialogic encounter and narrative exchange through conversations unfold meaning and help the individual understand agency and manoeuvre the vernacular, the social and the political contexts of personal and moral dilemmas. In this way, narrative itself becomes ethical discourse, and narrative encounter, a moral space. So far, we are claiming that learning through narrative is also learning within a community—through encounter, interaction and conversations with others. In this claim, we assume that learners are people who are resourceful and who can learn by being self-taught and who can contribute to other people's learning. Palmer (1998) argues that to learn in this way is to tap into the community of truth. We now offer a case study of what this process might look like for both the teacher/facilitator and the learners themselves.

The context of this case study is the Masters in Education Studies programme at a university in England. Scherto has been the facilitator of the programme since 2006. The M.A. is a flexible research-based degree, and most of the students are part-time mature students who are teachers, educators or persons who intend to facilitate others' learning in some way. The programme allows the participants to construct their own coherent integrated learning experience through group-based interaction, library-based individual work and empirical research in the field or inquiry at workplace. Core teaching of the programme is through seminars, group meetings and one-to-one supervision with a tutor. The M.A. starts with a self-inquiry into learning through the participants' writing of a learning biography. The project features both personal biographies and the interpretation and theorisation of learning.

The concept of learning biography used here is based on Dominicé's (2000) definition of educational biography, which is an interpretation made by an adult about his or her life journey in learning. This approach was also inspired by Dominicé's educational biography seminar design at the University of Geneva. As we discussed earlier, personal lived experiences concern time and historical period, and context and historical location. In studying learning, like any social practice, it is important to build in an understanding of the context, historical, social, cultural, political, in which that learning takes place. This means that life stories of learning as narrated individually are not sufficient to understand the social and historical context. Collaboration between the narrators of the stories through dialogue and interaction can be one way to achieve greater understanding of each lived experience. In this way, meaning is more likely to become intersubjective (Taylor, 1989).

To enable the participants to inquire into their life's journeys in learning, part of the programme includes:

1. The facilitator introduces the learning biography project to the group, including the intention of this project, the methodology of life history stories and biographical work, as well as the different learning theories and conceptualisations of learning. Literature about the use of life narratives in adult learning is also introduced to the group, with a few examples of other students' learning biography projects. Rich examples show the participants that there are no right or wrong ways of reflecting on personal narratives. Instead, they encourage the individuals' creativity and show respect for their ways of thinking and narrating.

2. Participants prepare (*pre-active* narrative process) and share oral narratives of their individual journeys in learning (*interactive* narrative encounter). This is the process of narration, involving the group paying careful attention to any experience relevant to learning as the participant perceives it, from childhood to the present, from formal learning, to informal, incidental and accidental learning. A key aspect of this sharing is that the teacher/facilitator is also offering his/her own personal narrative as a member of the group.

   Participants often bring in artefacts they have prepared for this occasion—these are mostly posters of timelines, drawings of learning journeys, personally significant objects, pieces of creative writing such as poems, and photos. The other aspect is participants' manner of engagement—at the narration level, the audiences are to be fully present, attentive in a quiet, open and receptive manner that allows the narrator to come forward with their own stories.

3. After the initial narration, participants provide and receive feedback to and from each other. This is where questions are raised and critical incidents and transitions are probed in a mutually supportive manner. This is the process of collaboration, and it requires each individual to be open to other journeys from the traveller's perspectives but to also develop critical self-reflection.

4. Then the participants begin to prepare a written draft narrative. Individuals make a selection of stories or vignettes that they would like to focus on in order to highlight the connections between their life experiences and the activities and learning that have been developed. The articulation of these connections serves as the basis for their theorisation about learning. This process involves dialogues with tutors and peers, collaborative interpretation and analysis so as to locate individual stories within their wider historical time and political contexts, social and cultural practices.

5. In a second workshop, the participants present their draft (written) narratives to the group. Theorisation follows as the result of analysis and interpretation, critical self-reflection, guided reading and a critical discussion of the literature. Although this process prioritises group work, participants also work closely with their supervisors/personal tutors on a one-to-one basis. Tutors suggest reading materials and help the participants move forward with theorisation.

6. The final completed learning biography (the *post-interactive* reflection and narrative *re-construction*) is structured to include the narrative vignettes, understanding and interpretation of the lived experiences in learning, analysis in the

light of theories about learning, and what the participant intends to focus on during the M.A. studies and classroom practices and beyond.

In this way, the final written assignment of the learning biography integrates the participants' learning from each of the above stages, capturing the richness of the narratives and constructing meaning from lived experience. Here we use Anne's narrative reconstruction to illustrate the importance of the dialogue and interchange with the group in shaping her understanding of her experience and how she sees her way forward.

Anne described her first moment of the process as the unanticipated opening of the emotional floodgates. She narrated her experience to a group of seven peers and Scherto, the facilitator. Anne used a timeline to assist her storytelling and her initial narrative was linear and mainly focused on her own educational experience as a learner and to a lesser extent, as an educator.

Growing up in the rural West Country of England, Anne had a happy 'free-range' childhood in the early sixties. She was an artistic and creative child—always drawing, and making beautiful things by hands. The awe and wonder of a star-gazing young girl's carefree life was a stark contrast to her early adolescence of confusion. The secondary school she attended was rigid, allowing little space for Anne to express her curiosity or explore the questions she had about herself and the world. This, compounded by the pain of being bullied at school, led to her disappointment with schooling. Depression crept up on her when she was fifteen. Her parents had to withdraw Anne from school and tried to home-educate her. This was when Anne had her first experience of self-education and using (unintentionally) art as a form of self-therapy. That seemed to help her step out of the darkness of depression.

Falling in love and getting married in her early 20s, to Anne, was the real gift of life. An Irish man from a working class upbringing and family of eleven, her husband was the emotional strength in her life, and this support gave her the courage to return to formal learning at the age of twenty-five. Due to having no prior qualifications such as A-Levels to prove her academic capabilities, Anne was placed on an 'Access' course to become acclimatised to academic studies. This made her feel nervous and somewhat fearful about what to expect from university life. Fear paralysed Anne when she started her undergraduate studies, and it took her almost five years to complete her first degree in psychology.

Before Anne was able to find employment with her new qualification, she entered a happy but challenging phase of her life: motherhood. While her daughter was growing up, Anne's fear of her daughter repeating her experience in schools overtook her. She decided to create a school that aimed at providing an ideal environment for her daughter and other children to thrive in. Unfortunately, this coincided with the introduction of the National Curriculum and SATs (Standard Attainment Tests) preparation becoming the focus of schooling. This development made it even harder to start a school run by parents that aimed at encouraging the children's own spirits and nurturing their curiosity. But Anne and others put together all the resources needed and for several years, the small school these parents founded was successful and became a home to a few dozen children and their families. However, the good times did not last, and eventually the school lost its appeal to continue to use the site which was being bought by a real estate developer and was forced to close down.

Following the school's closure, Anne and her family moved from their rural home to a seaside city, and whilst she experienced the strangeness of a new place, she was also excited by the many new prospects possible due to the openness in people's attitude, and the richness and diversity of cultures in the more cosmopolitan environment. At this juncture, Anne was introduced to the possibility of studying for the M.A. by a friend who also gave Anne the renewed strength and aspiration to return to formal learning. But she was once again confronted with that fear of academic studies and doubted if she had the capacity to make the grade.

The group's initial response after Anne's narration was silence. As each person absorbed the emotions in Anne's stories, there seemed, at the same time, to be a deeper and more reflexive process that each person was undergoing. Here, how others understood Anne's own conception of her learning journeys was equally important to her understanding of herself and how she would express herself through learning and doing.

After some quiet reflection, questions were posed to Anne inviting her to give more details about the different episodes in her stories and about key incidents. At the initial narration stage, as a ground rule, the group engaged with Anne in a non-directional way. In other words, at this level, the role of the group was to help Anne to better understand her own experience from where she was, rather than imposing an interpretation on her experience. Questions and comments posed to Anne included: 'Would you explain a bit more how you taught yourself during home schooling? What did it make you feel about yourself?' or 'Would you tell us the reason why you chose to study psychology?' or 'Was it your undergraduate studies that helped you develop the ethos of the small school? If so, how?' and so on. Narration was a space where Anne's stories were received, listened to and explored with respect.

After each participant had narrated their experience and had the opportunity for some initial un-directed probing, the group entered the collaboration phrase and further mutual exploration of meaning and direction, as illustrated in Chapter Seven. Through these collaborative endeavours, Anne and her peers suggested there was a persistent theme running through all her stories—whenever her life reached a transition, Anne seemed to have an unyielding desire to pursue learning or be propelled to embark on some kind of learning journey, formal or informal, as well as self-directed. Anne was surprised by this interpretation as she was struggling with her own dilemma about education. On the one hand, she seriously doubted that the way learning is facilitated in formal educational settings can actually allow any space for individual development as it seems all the emphasis is on subject knowledge rather than the development of the person; on the other hand, she was convinced that formal learning, through schooling, higher education within the university, is indeed crucial for individual growth, if facilitated well. Yet, the bitterness of her early study experiences and the fear of failure she experienced preoccupied her mind and impeded her from engaging fully in the learning itself.

The group shared Anne's anxiety about learning in general but also the opportunities it might open up for personal development. As Anne went deeper into understanding her experience, each participant also explored key dimensions in their own lives. According to Palmer (1998), this kind of process is not aimed at solving problems, rather it is sowing the seeds for growth. Listening to each other and to oneself is the key to narrative learning within a community.

As a participant on the M.A. programme, Anne's oral learning biography was only a start. She went on to write down these selected vignettes, which were then developed into a learning biography, and the written comments and feedback from her peers and tutors continued this social process of self-exploration. Further conversations with her personal tutor consolidated Anne's understanding of learning but also served to reassure Anne about her capacity to pursue learning within an academic institution. The final learning biography saw Anne's theorisation focused on an unyielding quest for truth—curiosity and motivation which involves commitment and emotional attachment—as the spark for lifelong learning. Learning, as conceptualised by Anne, is a 'formative process involving the experience of being human as in living consciously and fully in the moment, and progressing along the path to authentic human becoming' (extract from Anne's learning biography).

Sharing personal learning biography in a group also allowed Anne to reexamine her focus of study during the M.A. and her professional life beyond. Anne did not have a conventional teaching qualification and at the time of taking the M.A., she was not working in an educational institution. These contributed to her uncertainty about what to do during and after the M.A. Being in a group gave Anne the privilege of 'thinking aloud' about this with her peers, who offered to listen and give Anne the support she needed in order to come to a good understanding of her own stories to date and her direction for the future. Anne's decision was to focus her research on the effect of art activities on children's emotional and social development in secondary education. To do this, Anne volunteered in a local school in a deprived area of the city and created an art programme for young people with challenging behaviours. Eventually, this led to her setting up a successful charity that offers such programmes to local schools.

Anne and her peers called this one of their unfolding stories. Indeed, the narrative process allows these individuals to change their stories; at the same time, the new meaning and interpretation engendered offers an opportunity for them to change as persons. The unfolding stories of teachers and educators seem connected to helping the learners to achieve their potential and wellbeing.

Teachers' writing learning biographies collaboratively is a form of self-study, which facilitates a narrative process of looking inwardly and reflexively at oneself, which in turn, makes it possible to look outward and be open to others. Thus the teachers were able to develop an enhanced understanding of themselves, their profession, learners, and their needs within a social and political context. This process makes their concerns more explicit—to commit their teaching and learning to the good—the good for themselves as teachers, the good for the learner, and the good for the wider world.

3. The power of narrative—living in a community

Many scholars view narrative as a broad concept, not just limited to the personal experiences and stories of individuals. As we discussed earlier in this book, narrative can be a more general term, including memories, myths, missions, dreams, stories, histories, beliefs, religions and faith traditions, values, concepts, images, practices, sexuality, politics, institutions, interpretations and theories. They form an essential part of what shapes who we are and what we do in the world. At the same time, all human beings are brought up within certain narratives, so a person's understanding of him/herself and understanding of others also link to their narratives. Meanwhile narrative provides the frameworks for our understanding and also limits the possibility of our understanding. In this book, we have established that narrative is not a product or object of analysis and interpretation; rather it is a process of dialogic and reciprocal encounter (including encounters with the other, and the otherness of oneself) and learning.

Narrative is a powerful way of meaning-making in a community and an essential expression of being human and alongside with one another. Bringing groups together to share narratives honours the humanity within each of us as it engages people in encounters and openness through relationships and true listening. As we pointed out, ultimately, it is through the encounter that people are connected and a community takes shape.

Accordingly, Richard Kearney, in his conversation with Victor Taylor, explains how narrative imagination has an important role to play in the construction and administration of power politics. He says:

> the best response to destructive stories (which reduce otherness to sameness) is to counteract them with deconstructive stories—ones which undermine the illusory lure of fixated identity and open us to a process of narrative alternation and mutation (the self-as-another or *ipse*). . . . Stories can undo stories. Narratives that emancipate can respond to narratives that paralyze and incarcerate. History is full of such conflicting stories, as is psychoanalysis and religion. So why should politics be exempt from this complex play of narrative imaginaries? It is not (Kearney & Taylor, 2005, p. 21).

Whitebrook (2001) on the other hand, sees narrative identity as situated and embedded in a political context. She writes:

> For any given person, their identity is somewhat a political matter: they operate— or not—in a political world, their identity is affirmed, recognized, in part by their political status or activity, their (potential) behaviour as a political actor (p. 140).

Both support a view that narrative is never limited to the individual. It is at the same time social, historical and political. Even when narrative as a form of self-study, it can lead to individual and collective social action (Pithouse, Mitchell, & Moletsane, 2009). This view is similar to the example we offered above. In this way, narrative work points towards implications way beyond the personal as it can impact on social policies, political actions, and wider educational and political reforms.

One powerful example to show that narrative unites the social, cultural, historical and the political is the use of narrative in the post-conflict reconciliation process and in healing divided societies and communities. According to Gobodo-Madikizela & Van Der Merwe (2009), narrative plays a crucial part in healing human and political trauma, and can serve as the basis for dialogue and negotiating the changing role of memories in the aftermath of violence. Narrative offers an important opportunity for individuals and communities to hear each other's stories and their memories of pain and suffering but also allows mourning, repentance and asking for and offering forgiveness. In the Latin American Truth Commissions, the narratives of the victims were included; the Truth and Reconciliation Commissions in South Africa encouraged narratives from both victims and perpetrators. Other post-conflict reconciliation programmes have offered opportunities for the stories from victims, perpetrators, witnesses and bystanders, their families, and communities to be heard. Narratives about past experience and memories can enable people to see others in the context of their emotions and motivation, to understand the complex webs of relationships, and above all, to see other as fellow human beings. Seeking narrative truth places a human face on the other and allows the individual to embark on a journey of discovering and understanding–an understanding of how these past events and memories affect the ways individuals think about who they are.

However, the narrative process in post-conflict transformation does not stop at where the persons and the groups have come to terms with the past and listen to the stories from the opposite sides of history. The nature of the narrative process and the power of profound encounter as explored in this book make it possible for divided communities to come together and seek a common path towards a mutual future. The re-constructed and shared narrative is the foundation for that future.

Some may argue that this process resembles narrative therapy or most therapeutic work in that it empowers the individuals to heal themselves through re-constructing their personal narratives in a respectful and caring manner. It draws upon the rich resources individuals have, such as their skills, competences, beliefs, values, commitment, and above all, the capacity to resolve problems in their own lives. White & Espton (1990) would further point out that the narrative pedagogy described in this book links closely to that of narrative therapy in the sense that they both share the common element of facilitation through questioning, conversations and the authentic engagement of the interlocutors.

However, elsewhere, we pointed out that there is a clear distinction between the way that life narratives are explored as pedagogy and as therapy. Gill (2009) maintains that the fundamental difference lies in the following two aspects: first, when the narrative process serves as a site and space for pedagogic encounters, unlike in narrative therapy, the narrator is not perceived as 'ill' or 'wounded' and waiting to be treated and healed; nor is there a problem in the person's life which needs to be resolved. Second, the purpose of narrative encounter is learning, and to a greater extent, reciprocal learning. In contrast, narrative as therapy intends to explore stories in order to understand problems and their effects on a person's life–and provide solutions based on specific diagnoses. Consequently, narrative as a learning pursuit is different from narrative used in psychotherapy.

Yet it is undoubtedly the case that as we can see, in all of the case studies included in this book, the importance of therapeutic sensitivity and emotional empathy.

We also recognise that narrative pedagogy often has a therapeutic effect (Lieblich, McAdams, & Josselson, 2004). The point really at issue here is the degree to which narrative encounters depend on the hierarchy of specialised expertise of pre-codified knowledge. It is the way that this is invoked and utilised that is the key to understanding how the encounter works. Most of the examples offered in this book suggest that the more individuals approach each other with a sense of equality, a sense of the vernacular, with the willingness to listen intently to each other, the more this is likely to be an empowering and pedagogic relationship.

4. Narrative pedagogy—a review of our journey so far

As we mentioned earlier, this book reflects a belief in an underlying spiral process in our own learning and understanding. Now in the last section of the last chapter of the book, it is a good time to re-visit our own journey and our conversations and review our own learning and understanding.

First, this book brought together relevant concepts and conceptualisations of life narrative and placed them together in order to clarify the relationships between narrative, learning and personhood. We did so in the light of postmodernist interpretations. These reviews helped us to point out the postmodernist dilemma in understanding identity and selfhood, in that the more 'decentred', 'fragmented', 'multiple', and 'shifting' the self is, the more urgent the need to develop some kind of coherence towards meaningful and united actions in the future.

This leads to the second endeavour of this book—to establish the importance of narrative in human life and in social research. We argued that the nature of narrative invites personal engagement from the researchers in ways that are biographically meaningful for them. We have managed to address the concerns we have in the field, in particular, in terms of social research through in-depth narrative and life history interviews serving as a significant form of an intervention in the flow of a person's life. Rather than hiding behind the idea of 'distance', 'objectivity' and other models of research ethics, we suggest that it is necessary to become 'up close and personal' and embrace relationships in narrative and life history work.

A closer examination of the manners individuals have adopted in their narrative telling gave us the opportunity to further develop the notion of narrative capacity that Ivor and colleagues have started to analyse through the Learning Lives project. Our analysis enabled us to present this as a spectrum of different kinds of narrativity. This analysis is particularly important as it provides a framework for us to sensitise the life storytellers' learning potentials.

Although we might be able characterise the individual's narrative capacities in a broad spectrum, narrative process itself is not proceduralisable. Good intention is important and creating a trusting and spiritual space is the key to an open atmosphere where individuals feel comfortable about sharing their lived experiences in narratives. This is where we encounter each other as human beings on many levels: cognitive, discursive, emotional and spiritual.

Narrative encounter and elaboration involve the crafting and re-crafting of a personalised vision of life linked to a course of action, which is then invested with personal commitment, ownership and agency. Thus narrative is an ideal pedagogic site for facilitating learning and personal development. The main task of this book was to investigate the nature of narrative encounter and develop the theory of narrative pedagogy. Due to differentiated individual narrative capacities, narrative pedagogy would differ substantially accordingly. An understanding of key ingredients involved in the narrative encounter offers an invaluable opportunity to re-examine the notion of pedagogy from a deeper level. We have arrived at such conclusions that narrative pedagogy is situated within a deep and caring relationship between the educator/teacher/facilitator and the learner, and the reciprocity in learning as well as bound up with the educator's identity and integrity.

From the point of view of developing narrative pedagogy is the intersection of two interfaces: the first is between the symbolic/mental order of the personal narrative and the development of courses of action to be implemented in the material world. This relationship is complex and each person develops a different balancing of those two forces. The narrative encounter at the heart of narrative pedagogy works at this point to balance and to develop a self-actualising course of action.

A second interface is between the individual personal narrative and collective/societal narratives. Often personal development works best when there are degrees of harmonisation with wider social narratives. For instance a teacher concerned to make 'Every Child Matters' a reality and implement inclusive pedagogy would work with such grain of those societal narratives centring on justice and equality. Similarly a person living in a society characterised by past or present conflict might work with individual and collective notions of reconciliation. Hence a personal narrative involving reconciliation with self and surroundings might prove most efficacious when linked to those narratives of the communities and social forces pursuing peace and reconciliation.

However, whilst internal reflection and individual reconciliation are important in their own right, they must work in alliance with the analyses of the external contexts. It is always an individual 'story of action within a theory of context'. As Marx[1] wrote, man makes their own history, . . . but they do not make it under circumstances of their own choosing. Women and men must have a sense of making their own (his)story but accompanied by ongoing appraisal of circumstances and social contexts in which they are embedded.

In many ways these views about the relationship between the individual and society almost invert the established dictum that *the personal is political*. In the current world of deracinated politics and corporate override of democratic forms, we feel *the political is personal*. What this would mean in the example of conflict resolution noted above is that patterns of social resolution would have to grow from the bottom up, i.e., from patterns of individual reconciliation. It is difficult to envisage major national reconciliation without the broad-based reconciliation at the individual level.

This takes us back to the route from narration through to developing integrity. Self-actualisation depends on and derives from the capacity to move from the symbolic/mental construction of a narrative to the definition and delineation of action in the everyday world. At its heart, narrative pedagogy aims at employing strategies to empower people and expand their capacity to move from the internal affairs of narrative construction to the 'external relations' with others and with the wider world.

In the lifelong development of linkages between internal narrative constructions and the person's actions in the world we can see how integrity is really a learning disposition. Narrative pedagogy can build on such learning dispositions but often interventions are carried on after the event. The person continues on the learning trajectory that the pedagogic encounters help focus or clarify. Narrative pedagogy then has a pro-active predisposing setting and a sustained reflective afterlife where maintaining integrity becomes an ongoing goal.

Questions for discussion

In this last chapter of the book we wanted to reinstate our point about the relationship between narrative learning and the moral self—it is not our intention to moralise or suggest that it is necessary to impose some kind of moral judgement on individuals and their behaviours. Narrative learning is ultimately connected to pursuing the wellbeing of the individual, and the wellbeing of their communities.

Whilst a good deal of the work in this book has focused on the pedagogic encounter as a one-to-one, face-to-face, interaction it is also an eminently social and collective process at heart. Hence in this chapter we have looked at, albeit too briefly, its role in collective settings. In our next book *Narrative and Critical Pedagogy*, we intend to explore this collective dimension in greater detail. In this chapter the example we offered of work with students of a Masters' programme in developing a learning biography is hopefully instructive. We wanted to show the potential of this capacity for learning in a collective milieu to generate new insights and understandings.

Narrative pedagogy draws heavily on the teacher/educator's identity and integrity. When Desmond Tutu was asked how he had encouraged the victims and perpetrators in Northern Ireland to share narratives in a most transformative way, he pointed to the light bulb and said: 'By switching on!' Similarly, narrative educators also draw from personal, emotional, social and spiritual resources in order to facilitate the safe, trusting and inspirational space for narrative learning. This process in itself is profound learning for the teacher/educator.

A few more questions can perhaps further expand on our thinking on the major concerns that this book set out to explore:

- Having explored the benefits of embedding narrative learning in a teacher education Masters' programme, what are the other possible avenues and opportunities for higher education to create space for intensive narrative encounter?

- Can narrative pedagogy be employed in the education of children? Why and why not?

- Auto/biographies have been used in many adult learning situations. Can you think of an example of such work and compare it with the work of learning biography: what are the similarities? What are the differences?

- How can biographical work (similar to the example of learning biography) help generate collective understandings and lead to a re-shaping of community relations?

Further Readings

Dean, R. G. (1998). A narrative approach to groups. *Clinical Social Work Journal, 26*(1), 23–37.

Denzin, N. (1989). *Interpretive biography*. London: Sage.

Gilmore, L. (2001). *The limits of autobiography: Trauma and testimony*. Ithaca, NY: Cornell University Press.

Newton, A. (1995). *Narrative ethics*. Cambridge, MA: Harvard University Press.

Nussbaum, M. (1990). *Love's knowledge: Essays on philosophy and literature*. New York: Oxford University Press.

Tonkin, E. (1992). *Narrating our pasts: The social construction of oral history*. Cambridge, UK: Cambridge University Press.

Whitebrook, M. (2001). *Identity, narrative and politics*. London: Routledge.

Notes

Chapter 1 Notes: The Concept of Narrative

1. Although this book does not allow us to pursue the performance of identity in more detail, we certainly recognise the importance of such body of work as in Goffman's, Butler's and others' writing, and see this as a significant area for future investigation in relation to narration and life history.
2. We want to thank our friend and colleague Garrett Thomson for sharing his thoughts on these challenges.

Chapter 2 Notes: The Narrative Turn in Social Research

1. There are more critiques of positivism in Cohen, Mannion & Morrison, 2000; Habermas, 1971.
2. From this point onward, we will use the general term 'narrative and life history' to refer to an over-arching genre of work involving a rigorous and collaborative process of narrative meaning-making. It does not exclude narrative inquiries or narrative research that fall into a similar category.

Chapter 5 Note: The Nature of Narrative Encounters

1. For a more thorough discussion on the topic, please refer to Hogan, 2000.

Chapter 8 Note: Narrative: Learning and Living in the Community

1. Karl Marx (1852), *The Eighteenth Brumaire of Louis Napoleon*

References

Allen, S. (2002). Reflection/refraction of the dying light: Narrative vision in nineteenth-century Russian and French fiction. *Comparative Literature*, (Winter 2002).

Anderson, N. (1923). *The hobo: The sociology of the homeless man.* Chicago: University of Chicago Press.

Arendt, A. (1958). *The human condition.* Chicago: University of Chicago Press.

Atkinson, P. (1997). Narrative turn or blind alley? *Qualitative Health Research*, *7*(3), 325–344.

Bakhtin, M. (1981). *The dialogic imagination.* Austin: University of Texas Press.

Bakhtin, M. (1984). *Problems of Dostoevsky's poetics.* C. Emerson (Ed. & Trans.). Minneapolis, MN: University of Michigan Press.

Bar-On, B. (1993). Marginality and epistemic privilege. In L. Alcoff & E. Potter (Eds.). *Feminist epistemologies.* New York: Routledge.

Bar-On, R., & Parker, J. (2000). *The handbook of emotional intelligence: Theory, development, assessment, and application at home, school, and in the workplace.* San Francisco: Jossey-Bass.

Barthes, R. (1975). *The pleasure of the text.* New York: Hill & Wang.

Barthes, R. (1977). *Image, music, text.* New York: Hill & Wang.

Beattie, T. (2003). *Woman,* New Century Theology Series. London & New York: Continuum.

Becker, H. (1971). *Sociological work: Method and substance.* New Brunswick, NJ: Transaction.

Berger, R., & Quinney, R. (2004). *Storytelling sociology: Narrative as social inquiry.* Boulder, CO: Lynne Rienner.

Biesta, G. J. J., & Tedder, M. (2006). How is agency possible? Towards an ecological understanding of agency-as-achievement. Working paper 5. Exeter, UK: The Learning Lives Project.

Birren, J., & Cochran, K. (2001). *Telling the stories of life through guided autobiography groups.* Baltimore, MD: Johns Hopkins University Press.

Booker, C. (2004). *The seven basic plots: Why we tell stories.* London: Continuum.

Bornat, J. (2002). A second take: Revisiting interviews with a different purpose. *Oral History,* 31(1), 47–53.

Bourdieu, P. (1994). *Language and symbolic power.* Oxford: Polity.

Brooks, P. (1984). *Ready for the plot: Design and intention in narrative.* Cambridge, MA & London: Harvard University Press.

Bruner, J. (1985). Narrative and paradigmatic modes of thought. In E. Eisner (Ed.), *Learning and teaching the ways of knowing.* 84th Yearbook of the National Society of Education (pp. 99–115). Chicago: University of Chicago Press.

Bruner, J. (1990). *Acts of meaning: Four lectures on mind and culture.* Cambridge, MA: Harvard University Press.

Bulmer, M. (1984). *The Chicago school of sociology.* Chicago: University of Chicago Press.

Butler, J. (1990). *Gender trouble: Feminism and the subversion of identity.* New York: Routledge.

Butler, J. (1999). *Gender trouble: Feminism and the subversion of identity.* New York: Routledge.

Butler, R. (1963). The life review: An interpretation of reminiscence in the aged. *Psychiatry,* 26, 65–75.

Carr, D. (2000). *Professionalism and ethics in teaching.* London: Routledge.

Carter, K. (1993). The place of story in the study of teaching and teacher education. *Educational Researcher,* 22(1), 5–18.

Casey, K. (1995). The new narrative research in education. *Review of Research in Education,* 21, 211–253.

Castells, M. (1997). *The power of identity, the information age: Economy, society and culture* Vol. II. Cambridge, MA & Oxford, UK: Blackwell.

Chodorow, N. (1986). Toward a relational individualism: The mediation of self through psychoanalysis. In T. Heller, M. Sosua, & D. Wellberg (Eds.). *Reconstructing individualism* (pp. 197–207). Stanford, CA: Stanford University Press.

Christman, J. (2004). Narrative unity as a condition of personhood. *Metaphilosophy,* 35(5), 695–713.

Clandinin, D., & Connelly, M. (2000) *Narrative inquiry: Experience and story in qualitative research.* San Francisco: Jossey-Bass.

Cohen, L., Mannion, L. & Morrison, K. [E4](2000). *Research methods in education.* London: Routledge.

Cole, A. L., & Knowles, J. G. (2000). *Researching teaching: Exploring teacher development through reflexive inquiry.* Needham Heights, MA: Allyn & Bacon.

Cole, A., & Knowles, J. (Eds.). (2001). *Lives in context: The art of life history research.* Walnut Creek, CA: AltaMira.

Connelly, F., & Clandinin, D. (1990). Stories of experience and narrative inquiry. *Educational Researcher, 19*(5), 2–14.

Cortazzi, M. (1993) *Narrative Analysis. Falmer Social Research and Educational Studies Series: 12,* London: Falmer /Routledge.

Cortazzi, M., & Jin, L. (1996). Cultures of learning: Language classrooms in China. In H. Coleman (Ed.), *Society and the language classroom* (pp. 169–206). Cambridge, MA: Cambridge University Press.

Crapanzano, V. (1999). On dialogue. In T. Maranhão (Ed.), *The interpretation of dialogue* (pp. 269–291). Chicago: University of Chicago Press.

Czarniawska, B. (2004). *Narratives in social science research.* Thousand Oaks, CA: Sage.

Damasio, A. (1995). *Descartes's error: Emotion, reason, and the human brain.* New York: Putnam.

Day, C. (2004). *A passion for teaching.* London: RoutledgeFalmer.

Day, C. & Leitch, R. (2001). Teachers' and teacher educators' lives: The role of emotion. *Teaching and Teacher Education, 17*(4), 403–415.

Denzin, N. (1997). *Interpretative ethnography: Ethnographic practices for the 21st century.* Thousand Oaks, CA: Sage.

Denzin, N. (2004). Preface. In M. Andrews, S. D. Sclater, C. Squire, & A. Treacher (Eds.), *The uses of narrative.* New Jersey: Transaction.

Deslandes, J. (2004). A philosophy of emoting. *Journal of Narrative Theory, 34*(3), (Fall 2004), 335–372.

Dewey, J. (1916). *Democracy and education.* New York: Macmillan.

Dirkx, J. (1997). Nurturing soul in adult learning. In P. Cranton (Ed.), *Transformative learning in action: Insights from practice.* San Francisco: Jossey-Bass.

Dollard, J. (1949). *Criteria for the life history.* Magnolia, MA: Peter Smith.

Dominicé, P. (2000). *Learning from our lives: Using educational biographies with adults.* San Francisco: Jossey-Bass.

Elbaz, F. (1990). Knowledge and discourse: The evolution of research on teacher thinking. In C. Day, M. Pope, & P. Denicolo (Eds.), *Insights into teacher thinking and practice* (pp. 15–42). London: RoutledgeFalmer.

Epston, D., & White, M. (1990). *Narrative means to therapeutic ends.* New York: Norton.

Flood, G. (2000). Mimesis, narrative and subjectivity in the work of Girard and Ricoeur. *Journal for Cultural Research, 4*(2), 205–215.

Foucault, M. (1972). *Archaeology of knowledge.* New York: Pantheon.

Foucault, M. (1988). The political technology of individuals. In L. Martin, H. Gutman, & P. Hutton (Eds.), *Technologies of the self: A seminar with Michel Foucault* (pp. 145–163). London: Tavistock.

Freeman, M. (2007). Performing the event of understanding in hermeneutic conversations with narrative texts. *Qualitative Inquiry, 13*(7), 925–944.

Freire, P. (1970). *Pedagogy of the oppressed.* New York: Continuum.

Gadamer, H. -G. (1989). *Truth and method* (first published in 1960). New York: Seabury.

Gadamer, H. -G. (1977). *Philosophical hermeneutics.* David E. Linge (Trans. & Ed.). Berkeley, CA & Los Angeles, CA: University of California Press.

Geertz, C. (1983). Blurred genres: The refiguration of social thought. In C. Geertz (Ed.), *Local knowledge. Further essays in interpretive anthropology.* New York: Basic.

Gergen, K. J. (1996). Beyond life narratives in the therapeutic encounter. In J. E. Birren & G. M. Kenyon (Eds.), *Aging and biography: Explorations in adult development* (pp. 205–223). New York: Springer.

Gergen, K. (1998). Narrative, moral identity and historical consciousness: A social constructionist account. In In J. Straub (Ed.), *Identitat und historisches Bewusstsein.* Frankfurt: Suhrkamp. Retrieved fromhttp://www.swarthmore.edu/Documents/faculty/gergen/Narrative_Moral_Identity_and_Historical_Consciousness.pdf

Gibson, F. (1994). *Reminiscence and recall: A guide to good practice.* London: Age Concern England.

Giddens, A. (1990). *The consequences of modernity.* Cambridge, MA: Polity.

Giddens, A. (1991). *Modernity and self-identity. Self and society in the late modern age.* Cambridge, MA: Polity.

Gill, S. (2005). *Learning across cultures* (unpublished thesis). University of Sussex, East Sussex, UK.

Gill, S. (2007a). Overseas students' intercultural adaptation as intercultural learning: A transformative framework. *Journal of Comparative and International Education, 37,* 167–183.

Gill, S. (2007b). Engaging teachers' learning as whole person. Paper presented at SHRE Annual Conference, December 2007, Brighton, UK.

Gill, S. (Ed.). (2009). *Exploring selfhood: Finding ourselves, finding our stories in life narratives.* Brighton, UK: Guerrand-Hermès Foundation.

Gill, S. (2010). The homecoming: An investigation into the effect that studying overseas had on Chinese postgraduates' life and work on their return to China. *Journal of Comparative and International Education, 40*(3), 359–376.

Gill, S., & Goodson, I. (2010). Narrative and life history research. In B. Somakh & C. Lewin (Eds.), *Handbook of social research* (pp. 157–165). London: Sage.

Gill, S., & Thomson, G. (2009). *Human-centred education.* Brighton, UK: Guerrand-Hermès Foundation.

Gilligan, C. (1982). *In a different voice.* Cambridge, MA: Harvard University Press.

Glass, J. (1993). *Shattered selves: Multiple personality in a postmodern world.* Ithaca, NY: Cornell University Press.

Gobodo-Madikizela, P. & Van der Merwe, C. (2009). *Memory, narrative, and forgiveness: Perspectives on the unfinished journeys of the past.* New Castle, UK: Cambridge Scholars.

Gobodo-Madikizela, P. (2003). *A human being died that night: A South African story of forgiveness*. Boston, MA: Houghton Mifflin.

Goffman, E. (1959). *The presentation of self in everyday life*. Garden City, NY: Anchor.

Goleman, D. (1995). *Emotional intelligence*. New York: Bantam.

Goodson, I. (1991). Sponsoring the teacher's voice. *Cambridge Journal of Education,* Vol. 21, No. 1.

Goodson, I. (Ed.). (1992a). *Studying teachers' lives*. New York: Teachers College Press.

Goodson, I. (Ed.). (1992b). *Teachers' lives,* New York & London: Routledge.

Goodson, I. (1992c & 2005). *Learning, curriculum and life politics*. Abingdon: Routledge.

Goodson, I. (1995). The story so far: Personal knowledge and the political. *Qualitative Studies in Education*

Goodson, I. (2003). *Professional knowledge/professional lives*. London & New York: Open University Press.

Goodson, I. (2006). The rise of the life narrative. *Teachers Education Quarterly* (Fall 2006).

Goodson, I. (2010, forthcoming). *Developing narrative theory*. New York & London: Routledge.

Goodson, I., Biesta, G., Tedder, M., & Adair, N. (2010). *Narrative learning*. Abingdon: Routledge.

Goodson, I., & Sikes, P. (2001). *Life history in educational settings: Learning from lives*. Buckingham, UK: Open University Press.

Grassie[E9], W. (2008). *Entangled narratives: Competing visions of the good life*. Paper presented at a symposium of the US-Sri Lankan Fulbright Commission in Colombo, January 4, 2008.

Guba, E., & Lincoln, Y. (1994). Competing paradigms in qualitative research. In N. Denzin & Y. Lincoln (Eds.), *Handbook of qualitative research*. London: Sage.

Habermas, J. (1971). *Knowledge and human interests*. J. J. Shapiro (Trans.). Boston, MA: Beacon.

Halbwachs, M. (1980). *The collective memory*. F. Dulles & V. Ditter (Trans.). New York: Harper & Row.

Hargreaves, A., & Goodson, I. (1996a). Teachers' professional lives: Aspirations and actualities. In I. I. Goodson & A. Hargreaves (Eds.), *Teachers' professional lives* (pp. 1–27). Washington, DC: RoutledgeFalmer.

Hargreaves, A., & Goodson, I. (Eds.). (1996b). *Teachers' professional lives*. London; New York; & Philadelphia, PA: RoutledgeFalmer.

Hatch, J., & Wisniewski, R. (1995). Life history and narrative: Questions, issues and exemplary works. In J. A. Hatch & R. Wisniewski (Eds.), *Life history and narrative* (pp. 113–135). Washington, DC: RoutledgeFalmer.

Hayden, T. (1980). *One child*. New York: Avon.

Hayden, T. (1995). *Tiger's child*. New York: Avon.

Heinze, M. (2009). Affectivity and personality: Mediated by the social. *Philosophy, Psychiatry, & Psychology, 16*(3), 273–275.

Hekman, S. (2000). Beyond identity: Feminism, identity and identity politics. *Feminist Theory, 1,* 289–308.

Hendry, P. (2007). The future of narrative. *Qualitative inquiry, 13*(4), 487–498.

Herman, D., Jahn, M., & Ryan, M. (2005). *Routledge encyclopedia of narrative theory.* London: Routledge.

Heron, J. (1992). *Feeling and personhood: Psychology in another key.* London: Sage.

Hinchman, L., & Hinchman, S. (1997). *Memory, identity, community. The idea of narrative in the human sciences.* New York: SUNY Press.

Hitchcock, G., & Hughes, D. (1995). *Research and the teacher: A qualitative introduction to school-based research* (2nd ed.). London: Routledge.

Hogan, P. (2000). Gadamer and the philosophy of education. Encyclopedia of philosophy of education, Retrieved from http://www.ffst.hr/ENCYCLOPAEDIA/doku.php?id=gadamer_and_philosophy_of_education)

Hogan, P. (2003). *The mind and its stories: Narrative universals and human emotion.* Cambridge, MA: University of Cambridge Press.

Izard, C. (1991). *The psychology of emotions.* London & New York: Plenum.

Jack, D. (1991). *Silencing the self: Depression and women.* Cambridge, MA: Harvard University Press.

Jolly, M. (2001). *The encyclopaedia of life writing.* London & New York: Fitzroy Dearborn/Routledge.

Josselson, R. (1995). *The space between us: Exploring the dimensions of human relationships: Exploring dimensions of human relationships* (pp. xii/xiii). Thousand Oaks, CA: Sage.

Karpiak, I. (2003). The ethnographic, the reflective, and the uncanny: Three "tellings" of autobiography. *Journal of Transformative Education,* Vol. 1, No. 2, pp. 99–116.

Kearney, R., & Taylor, V. (2005). A conversation with Richard Kearney. *Journal for Cultural and Religious Theory, 6*(2), 17–26.

Knowles, J. (1993). Life-history accounts as mirrors: A practical avenue for the conceptualization of reflection in teacher education. In J. Calderhead & P. Gates (Eds.), *Conceptualizing reflection in teacher development* (pp. 70–98). London: RoutledgeFalmer.

Kolak, D., & Thomson, G. (2005). *The Longman standard history of philosophy* (w/G. Thomson). New York: Pearson/Longman.

Koschmann, T. (1999). *Toward a dialogic theory of learning: Bakhtin's contribution to understanding learning in settings of collaboration.* International Society of the Learning Sciences, 38.

Labov, W. (1972). *Language in the inner city.* Philadelphia, PA: University of Pennsylvania Press.

Labov, W. (1997). Some further steps in narrative analysis. *Journal of Narrative and Life History, 7,* 395–415.

Lazarus, R. (1991). *Emotion and adaptation.* Oxford: Oxford University Press.

Lieblich, A., McAdams, D., & Josselson, R. (Eds.). (2004). *Healing plots: The narrative basis of psychotherapy.* San Francisco: American Psychological Association.

Lyard, R., & Dunn, J. (2009). *A good childhood: Searching for values in a competitive age.* London: The Children's Society.

Lyon, D. (2000). *Postmodernity: Concepts in social thought.* Minneapolis, MN: University of Minnesota Press.

Lyotard, J. -F. (1984). The postmodern condition. Manchester, UK: Manchester University Press.

MacIntyre, A. (1981). Ideology, social science and revolution. *Comparative Politics, 5,* 321–341.

MacIntyre, A. (1984). *After virtue.* Notre Dame, IN: University of Notre Dame Press.

McAdams, D. (1993). *The stories we live by: Personal myths and the making of the self.* New York: Morrow.

McAdams, D. (1996). Personality, modernity, and the storied self: A contemporary framework for studying persons. Psychological Inquirymedium-normal>, 7medium-normal>, 295–321.

McAdams, D., Josselson, R., & Lieblich, A. (Eds.). (2006). *Identity and story: Creating self in narrative.* Washington, DC: APA.

Macmurray, J. (1961). *Persons in relations.* London: Faber.

Measor, L. & Sikes, P. (1992). Visiting lives: Ethics and methodology in life history. In I. Goodson (Ed.), *Studying teachers' lives* (pp. 209–233). New York: Teachers College Press.

Mezirow, J. (1978). *Education for perspective transformation: Women's re-entry programs in community colleges.* New York: Teachers College Press.

Mezirow, J. (1990). *Fostering critical reflection in adulthood. A guide to transformative and emancipatory learning.* San Francisco: Jossey-Bass.

Mezirow, J. (1991). *Transformative dimensions of adult learning.* San Francisco: Jossey-Bass.

Mezirow, J. (1995). Transformation theory of adult learning. In M. Welton (Ed.), *In defense of the life world.* New York: SUNY Press.

Mezirow, J. (Ed.). (2000). *Learning as transformation—critical perspectives on a theory in progress.* San Francisco: Jossey-Bass.

Miles, M., & Huberman, A. (1994). *Qualitative data analysis: An expanded sourcebook* (2nd ed.). Thousand Oaks, CA: Sage.

Muchmore, J. (2002). *Methods and ethics in a life history study of teacher thinking. The Qualitative Report, 7*(4), 1–18.

Myerhoff, B. (1992). *Remembered lives: The work of ritual, storytelling, and growing older.* Ann Arbor, MI: University of Michigan Press.

Noddings, N. (2010). Moral education in an age of globalization. *Educational Philosophy and Theory, 42*(4), 390–396.

Nussbaum, M. (1988), Nonrelative virtues: An Aristotelian approach. In P. French, T. Uehling, & H. Wettstein (Eds.), *Midwest studies in philosophy,* Vol. XIII: Ethical theory: Character and virtue. Notre Dame, IN: Notre Dame University Press.

Nussbaum, M. (1990). *Love's knowledge: Essays on philosophy and literature.* New York: Oxford University Press.

Oakley, A. (1981). Interviewing women: A contradiction in terms? In H. Roberts (Ed.), *Doing feminist research.* London: Routledge.

Ojermark, A. (2007). *Presenting life histories: A literature review and annotated bibliography.* CPRC Working Paper 101, Retrieved from http://www.chronicpoverty.org/uploads/pu blication_files/WP101_Ojermark.pdf

Palmer, P. (1998). *The courage to teach: Exploring the inner landscape of a teacher's life.* San Francisco: Jossey-Bass.

Park, R. (1952). *Human communities: The city and human ecology.* Glencoe, IL: Free Press.

Park, R., Burgess, E., & McKenzie, R. (1925). *The city.* Chicago: University of Chicago Press.

Pence, J. (2004). Narrative emotion: Feeling, form and function. *Journal of Narrative Theory, 34*(3), 273–276.

Pithouse, K., Mitchell, C., & Moletsane, R. (Eds.). (2009). *Making connections: Self-study & social action,* New York: Peter Lang.

Plummer, K. (1990). Herbert Blumer and the life history tradition. *Symbolic Interaction,* Vol 13, pp. 125–144.

Plummer, K. (2001). *Documents of life 2: An invitation to critical humanism.* London: Sage.

Polkinghorne, D. (1988). *Narrative knowing and the human sciences.* New York: SUNY Press.

Polkinghorne, D. (1995). Narrative configuration in qualitative analysis. In A. Hatch & R. Wisniewski (Eds.) *Life History and Narrative.* Washington: Falmer, pp. 5–23.

Ricoeur, P. (1984). *Time and narrative I.* Chicago: University of Chicago Press.

Ricoeur, P. (1988). *Time and narrative,* K. McLaughlin & D. Pellauer (Trans.). Chicago: University of Chicago Press.

Ricoeur, P. (1992). *Oneself as another.* K. Blamey (Trans.). Chicago: University of Chicago Press.

Riessman, C. (2005). Exploring ethics: A narrative about narrative research in South India. *Journal for the Social Study of Health, Illness and Medicine, 9*(4), 473–490.

Rogers, C. (1951) *Client-centered therapy: Its current practice, implications and theory.* Boston: Houghton Mifflin.

Rogers, C. (1969). *Freedom to learn: A view of what education might become.* Columbus, Ohio: Charles E. Merrill.

Rosfort, R., & Stanghellini, G. (2009). The feeling of being a person. *Philosophy, Psychiatry, & Psychology, 16*(3), 283–288.

Sarup, M. (1993). *An introductory guide to post-structuralism and postmodernism.* Atlanta, GA: University of Georgia Press.

Sarup, M. (1996). *Identity, culture, and the postmodern world.* . Atlanta, GA: University of Georgia Press.

Schweiker, W. (2004). A preface to ethics: Global dynamics and the integrity of life. *Journal of Religious Ethics, 32*(1), 13–38.

Sermijn, J., Devlieger, P., & Loots, G. (2008). The narrative construction of the self: Selfhood as a rhizomatic story. *Qualitative Inquiry, 14*(4), 632–650.

Shaw, C. (1930). *The jack-roller: A delinquent boy's own story*. Chicago: University of Chicago Press.

Sikes, P., Nixon, J., & Carr, W. (Eds.). (2003). *The moral foundations of educational research: Knowledge, inquiry and values*. Maidenhead, UK: Open University Press/McGraw Hill Educational.

Steedman, C. (1986). *Landscape for a good woman*. London: Virago.

Stones, R. (1996). *Sociological reasoning: Towards a post-modern sociology*. London: Macmillan.

Taylor, C. (1989). *Sources of the self: The making of the modern identity*. Cambridge, MA: Harvard University Press.

Taylor, C. (1991). *The ethics of authenticity*. Cambridge, MA. Harvard University Press.

Taylor, E. (1998). *The theory and practice of transformative learning: A critical review*. Columbus, OH: ERIC Clearinghouse on Adult, Career, and Vocational Education.

Tetlock, P. (1983). Accountability and complexity of thought. *Journal of Personality and Social Psychology, 45*(1), 74–83.

Thomas, W., & Znaniecki F. (1918–1920). *The Polish peasant in Europe and America: Monograph of an immigrant group*. Urbana, IL: University of Illinois Press.

Thomas, W., & Znaniecki, F. (1958). Methodological note. In Part I: Primary group organization of *The Polish peasant in Europe and America* I (pp. 1–86). New York: Dover.

Thomson, G. (1987). *Needs*. International Library of Philosophy series, London & New York: Routledge & Kegan Paul.

Thomson, G. (2002). *On the meaning of life*. Belmont, CA: Wadsworth.

Thrasher, F. (1927). *The gang*. Chicago: University of Chicago Press.

Turkle, S. (1995). *Life on the screen: Identity in the age of the Internet*. New York: Simon & Schuster.

Voloshinov, V. (1973). *Marxism and the philosophy of language*. Cambridge, MA: Harvard University Press.

Waks, L. (2010). *John Dewey on listening in school and society*. Paper presented at the Annual Conference of Society of Educational Philosophy, March 2010, Oxford.

Wenger, E. (1998). *Communities of practice: Learning, meaning, and identity*. Cambridge, MA: Cambridge University Press.

White, M., & Epston, D. (1990). *Narrative means to therapeutic ends*. New York: W. W. Norton.

Whitebrook, M. (2001). *Identity, narrative and politics*. London: Routledge.

Wirth, L. (1928). *The ghetto*. Chicago: University of Chicago Press.

Witherell, C. (1995). Narrative landscapes and the moral education: Taking the story to heart. In H. McEwan & K. Egan (Eds.), *Narrative in teaching, learning, and research*. (pp. 39–49). New York: Teachers College Press.

Witherell, C., & Noddings, N. (1991) *Stories lives tell: Narrative and dialogue in education.* New York: Teachers College Press.

Zorbaugh, H. (1929). *The Gold Coast and the slum: A sociological study of Chicago's. Near North Side.* Chicago: University of Chicago.

Index

Studies in the Postmodern Theory of Education

General Editor
Shirley R. Steinberg

Counterpoints publishes the most compelling and imaginative books being written in education today. Grounded on the theoretical advances in criticalism, feminism, and postmodernism in the last two decades of the twentieth century, Counterpoints engages the meaning of these innovations in various forms of educational expression. Committed to the proposition that theoretical literature should be accessible to a variety of audiences, the series insists that its authors avoid esoteric and jargonistic languages that transform educational scholarship into an elite discourse for the initiated. Scholarly work matters only to the degree it affects consciousness and practice at multiple sites. Counterpoints' editorial policy is based on these principles and the ability of scholars to break new ground, to open new conversations, to go where educators have never gone before.

For additional information about this series or for the submission of manuscripts, please contact:

Shirley R. Steinberg
c/o Peter Lang Publishing, Inc.
29 Broadway, 18th floor
New York, New York 10006

To order other books in this series, please contact our Customer Service Department:

(800) 770-LANG (within the U.S.)
(212) 647-7706 (outside the U.S.)
(212) 647-7707 FAX

Or browse online by series:
www.peterlang.com